The Birth of Tragedy

FRIEDRICH NIETZSCHE

Translated by Clifton P. Fadiman

DOVER PUBLICATIONS, INC.
New York

DOVER THRIFT EDITIONS

GENERAL EDITOR: STANLEY APPELBAUM

Bibliographical Note

This Dover edition, first published in 1995, contains the unabridged text of *The Birth of Tragedy from the Spirit of Music* as translated by Clifton P. Fadiman and published by the Modern Library, New York, in 1927 in *The Philosophy of Nietzsche*. A new Note has been written specially for the Dover edition.

Library of Congress Cataloging-in-Publication Data

Nietzsche, Friedrich Wilhelm, 1844–1900.
    [Geburt der Tragödie, English]
    The birth of tragedy / Friedrich Nietzsche.
        p.   cm. — (Dover thrift editions)
    "Contains the unabridged text of The birth of tragedy from the spirit of music as translated by Clifton P. Fadiman and published by the Modern Library, New York, in 1927 in The philosophy of Nietzsche"—T.p. verso.
    Includes bibliographical references.
    ISBN 0-486-28515-4
    1. Greek drama (Tragedy)—History and criticism. 2. Tragic, The. 3. Ethics. 4. Music—Philosophy and aesthetics. 5. Aesthetics. I. Title. II. Series.
B3313.G42E55 1995
111'.85—dc20
                                    95-10004
                                      CIP

Manufactured in the United States of America
Dover Publications, Inc., 31 East 2nd Street, Mineola, N.Y. 11501

Note

FRIEDRICH NIETZSCHE (1844–1900) stands among the most influential thinkers of modern times, having created a body of work that has had an effect extending far beyond the discipline of philosophy. It is ironical to note that Nietzsche, known for his critical attitude toward Christianity, came from a line of Lutheran ministers. His initial interest in theology was replaced by classical philology, for which he manifested such ability that he was offered a chair in Basel before he had won his doctorate. But Nietzsche's enthusiasm for philology waned and, although he continued to teach until 1879, his interest shifted to the broader field of philosophy. His first major work was that presented here, *The Birth of Tragedy (Die Geburt der Tragödie)*, 1872. The Foreword is addressed to Richard Wagner, to whose music dramas Nietzsche looked for a rebirth of tragedy. The relationship, however, became strained, and collapsed completely with the composition of *Parsifal*, which Nietzsche regarded as a genuflection to Christianity. In *The Birth of Tragedy*, setting forth the concept of the Apollonian and Dionysian, Nietzsche begins a reexamination of traditional values that he further developed in such works as *Thus Spake Zarathustra, Beyond Good and Evil, On the Genealogy of Morals* and *Ecce Homo*. In 1889 Nietzsche, whose physical health had long been precarious, began a mental decline that ended in madness and death.

Foreword to
Richard Wagner

In order to keep at a distance all the possible scruples, excitements, and misunderstandings to which the thoughts gathered in this essay will give occasion, considering the peculiar character of our esthetic publicity; and also that I may be able to write the introductory remarks with the same contemplative joy, whose reflection (the result of good and elevating hours) it bears on every page; that I may do this, I picture the moment when you, my much respected friend, will receive this essay; perhaps, after an evening walk in the winter snow, you will behold the unbound Prometheus on the title-page, read my name, and be at once convinced that, whatever this essay may contain, the author has something serious and impressive to say, and, moreover, that in all his meditations he communed with you as with one present and so could write only what befitted that presence. Thus you will be reminded that I collected myself for these thoughts just when your magnificent dissertation on Beethoven originated, amid the horrors and sublimities of the war which had just then broken out. But it would be a mistake for any to suppose that this collection merely opposes esthetic revelry to patriotic excitement, gay dilettanteism to gallant earnestness. Upon a real perusal of this essay, such a reader, rather to his surprise, will discover how serious is the German problem we must deal with, which we properly place, as the critical consideration, in the very center of German hopes. Perhaps, however, this same class of readers will be shocked at seeing an esthetic problem taken so seriously, especially if they see in art nothing but a merry diversion, an easily dispensed-with tinkling accompaniment to the "seriousness of existence": as if no one had any idea of the meaning of the opposition implied. These earnest ones may be informed of my conviction that art is the highest task and the proper metaphysical activity of this life, as it is understood by the man, to whom, as my noble champion on this same path, I now dedicate this essay.

Basel, *end of the year*, 1871.

WE shall do a great deal for the science of esthetics, once we perceive not merely by logical inference, but with the immediate certainty of intuition, that the continuous development of art is bound up with the *Apollonian* and *Dionysian* duality: just as procreation depends on the duality of the sexes, involving perpetual strife with only periodically intervening reconciliations. The terms Dionysian and Apollonian we borrow from the Greeks, who disclose to the discerning mind the profound mysteries of their view of art, not, to be sure, in concepts, but in the impressively clear figures of their gods. Through Apollo and Dionysus, the two art-deities of the Greeks, we come to recognize that in the Greek world there existed a sharp opposition, in origin and aims, between the Apollonian art of sculpture, and the non-plastic, Dionysian, art of music. These two distinct tendencies run parallel to each other, for the most part openly at variance; and they continually incite each other to new and more powerful births, which perpetuate an antagonism, only superficially reconciled by the common term "Art"; till at last, by a metaphysical miracle of the Hellenic will, they appear coupled with each other, and through this coupling eventually generate the art-product, equally Dionysian and Apollonian, of Attic tragedy.

In order to grasp these two tendencies, let us first conceive of them as the separate art-worlds of *dreams* and *drunkenness*. These physiological phenomena present a contrast analogous to that existing between the Apollonian and the Dionysian. It was in dreams, says Lucretius, that the glorious divine figures first appeared to the souls of men; in dreams the great shaper beheld the splendid corporeal structure of superhuman beings; and the Hellenic poet, if questioned about the mysteries of poetic inspiration, would likewise have suggested dreams and he might have given an explanation like that of Hans Sachs in the *Mastersingers*:

> "*Mein Freund, das grad' ist Dichters Werk,*
> *dass er sein Träumen deut' und merk'.*
> *Glaubt mir, des Menschen wahrster Wahn*

wird ihm im Traume aufgethan:
all' Dichtkunst und Poëterei
ist nichts als Wahrtraum-Deuterei."[1]

The beautiful appearance of the dream-worlds, in creating which every man is a perfect artist, is the prerequisite of all plastic art, and in fact, as we shall see, of an important part of poetry also. In our dreams we delight in the immediate apprehension of form; all forms speak to us; none are unimportant, none are superfluous. But, when this dream-reality is most intense, we also have, glimmering through it, the sensation of its appearance: at least this is my experience, as to whose frequency, aye, normality, I could adduce many proofs, in addition to the sayings of the poets. Indeed, the man of philosophic mind has a presentiment that underneath this reality in which we live and have our being, is concealed another and quite different reality, which, like the first, is an appearance; and Schopenhauer actually indicates as the criterion of philosophical ability the occasional ability to view men and things as mere phantoms or dream-pictures. Thus the esthetically sensitive man stands in the same relation to the reality of dreams as the philosopher does to the reality of existence; he is a close and willing observer, for these pictures afford him an interpretation of life, and it is by these processes that he trains himself for life. And it is not only the agreeable and friendly pictures that he experiences in himself with such perfect understanding: but the serious, the troubled, the sad, the gloomy, the sudden restraints, the tricks of fate, the uneasy presentiments, in short, the whole Divine Comedy of life, and the Inferno, also pass before him, not like mere shadows on the wall — for in these scenes he lives and suffers — and yet not without that fleeting sensation of appearance. And perhaps many will, like myself, recall that amid the dangers and terrors of dream-life they would at times, cry out in self-encouragement, and not without success. "It is only a dream! I will dream on!" I have likewise heard of persons capable of continuing one and the same dream for three and even more successive nights: facts which indicate clearly that our innermost beings, our common subconscious experiences, express themselves in dreams because they must do so and because they take profound delight in so doing.

This joyful necessity of the dream-experience has been embodied by the Greeks in their Apollo: for Apollo, the god of all plastic energies, is at

---

[1] "My friend, that is exactly the poet's task, to mark his dreams and to attach meanings to them. Believe me, man's most profound illusions are revealed to him in dreams; and all versifying and poetizing is nothing but an interpretation of them."

the same time the soothsaying god. He, who (as the etymology of the name indicates) is the "shining one," the deity of light, is also ruler over the fair appearance of the inner world of fantasy. The higher truth, the perfection of these states in contrast to the incompletely intelligible everyday world, this deep consciousness of nature, healing and helping in sleep and dreams, is at the same time the symbolical analogue of the soothsaying faculty and of the arts generally, which make life possible and worth living. But we must also include in our picture of Apollo that delicate boundary, which the dream-picture must not overstep — lest it act pathologically (in which case appearance would impose upon us as pure reality). We must keep in mind that measured restraint, that freedom from the wilder emotions, that philosophical calm of the sculptor-god. His eye must be "sunlike," as befits his origin; even when his glance is angry and distempered, the sacredness of his beautiful appearance must still be there. And so, in one sense, we might apply to Apollo the words of Schopenhauer when he speaks of the man wrapped in the veil of Mâyâ:[2] *Welt als Wille und Vorstellung*, I. p. 416: "Just as in a stormy sea, unbounded in every direction, rising and falling with howling mountainous waves, a sailor sits in a boat and trusts in his frail barque: so in the midst of a world of sorrows the individual sits quietly, supported by and trusting in his *principium individuationis*." In fact, we might say of Apollo, that in him the unshaken faith in this *principium* and the calm repose of the man wrapped therein receive their sublimest expression; and we might consider Apollo himself as the glorious divine image of the *principium individuationis*, whose gestures and expression tell us of all the joy and wisdom of "appearance," together with its beauty.

In the same work Schopenhauer has depicted for us the terrible *awe* which seizes upon man, when he is suddenly unable to account for the cognitive forms of a phenomenon, when the principle of reason, in some one of its manifestations, seems to admit of an exception. If we add to this awe the blissful ecstasy which rises from the innermost depths of man, aye, of nature, at this very collapse of the *principium individuationis*, we shall gain an insight into the nature of the *Dionysian*, which is brought home to us most intimately perhaps by the analogy of *drunkenness*. It is either under the influence of the narcotic draught, which we hear of in the songs of all primitive men and peoples, or with the potent coming of spring penetrating all nature with joy, that these Dionysian emotions awake, which, as they intensify, cause the subjective to vanish

---

[2] Cf. *World as Will and Idea*, I. 455 ff., trans. by Haldane and Kemp, 6th ed.

into complete self-forgetfulness. So also in the German Middle Ages singing and dancing crowds, ever increasing in number, were whirled from place to place under this same Dionysian impulse. In these dancers of St. John and St. Vitus, we rediscover the Bacchic choruses of the Greeks, with their early history in Asia Minor, as far back as Babylon and the orgiastic Sacæa. There are some, who, from obtuseness, or lack of experience, will deprecate such phenomena as "folkdiseases," with contempt or pity born of the consciousness of their own "healthy-mindedness." But, of course, such poor wretches can not imagine how anemic and ghastly their so-called "healthy-mindedness" seems in contrast to the glowing life of the Dionysian revellers rushing past them.

Under the charm of the Dionysian not only is the union between man and man reaffirmed, but Nature which has become estranged, hostile, or subjugated, celebrates once more her reconciliation with her prodigal son, man. Freely earth proffers her gifts, and peacefully the beasts of prey approach from desert and mountain. The chariot of Dionysus is bedecked with flowers and garlands; panthers and tigers pass beneath his yoke. Transform Beethoven's "Hymn to Joy" into a painting; let your imagination conceive the multitudes bowing to the dust, awestruck — then you will be able to appreciate the Dionysian. Now the slave is free; now all the stubborn, hostile barriers, which necessity, caprice or "shameless fashion" have erected between man and man, are broken down. Now, with the gospel of universal harmony, each one feels himself not only united, reconciled, blended with his neighbor, but as one with him; he feels as if the veil of Mâyâ had been torn aside and were now merely fluttering in tatters before the mysterious Primordial Unity. In song and in dance man expresses himself as a member of a higher community; he has forgotten how to walk and speak; he is about to take a dancing flight into the air. His very gestures bespeak enchantment. Just as the animals now talk, just as the earth yields milk and honey, so from him emanate supernatural sounds. He feels himself a god, he himself now walks about enchanted, in ecstasy, like to the gods whom he saw walking about in his dreams. He is no longer an artist, he has become a work of art: in these paroxysms of intoxication the artistic power of all nature reveals itself to the highest gratification of the Primordial Unity. The noblest clay, the most costly marble, man, is here kneaded and cut, and to the sound of the chisel strokes of the Dionysian world-artist rings out the cry of the Eleusinian mysteries: "Do ye bow in the dust, O millions? Do you divine your creator, O world?"

2

THUS far we have considered the Apollonian and its antithesis, the Dionysian, as artistic energies which burst forth from nature herself, *without the mediation of the human artist*; energies in which nature's art-impulses are satisfied in the most immediate and direct way: first, on the one hand, in the pictorial world of dreams, whose completeness is not dependent upon the intellectual attitude or the artistic culture of any single being; and, on the other hand, as drunken reality, which likewise does not heed the single unit, but even seeks to destroy the individual and redeem him by a mystic feeling of Oneness. With reference to these immediate art-states of nature, every artist is an "imitator," that is to say, either an Apollonian artist in dreams, or a Dionysian artist in ecstasies, or finally — as for example in Greek tragedy — at once artist in both dreams and ecstasies: so we may perhaps picture him sinking down in his Dionysian drunkenness and mystical self-abnegation, alone, and apart from the singing revelers, and we may imagine how now, through Apollonian dream-inspiration, his own state, *i.e.*, his oneness with the primal nature of the universe, is revealed to him in a *symbolical dream-picture*.

So much for these general premises and contrasts. Let us now approach the *Greeks* in order to learn how highly these *art-impulses of nature* were developed in them. Thus we shall be in a position to understand and appreciate more deeply that relation of the Greek artist to his archetypes, which, according to the Aristotelian expression, is "the imitation of nature." In spite of all the dream-literature and the numerous dream-anecdotes of the Greeks, we can speak only conjecturally, though with reasonable assurance, of their *dreams*. If we consider the incredibly precise and unerring plastic power of their eyes, together with their vivid, frank delight in colors, we can hardly refrain (to the shame of all those born later) from assuming even for their dreams a certain logic of line and contour, colors and groups, a certain pictorial sequence reminding us of their finest bas-reliefs, whose perfection would certainly justify us, if a comparison were possible, in designating the dreaming Greeks as Homers and Homer as a dreaming Greek: in a deeper sense than that in which modern man, speaking of his dreams, ventures to compare himself with Shakespeare.

On the other hand, there is no conjecture as to the immense gap which separates the *Dionysian Greek* from the Dionysian barbarian.

From all quarters of the Ancient World, — to say nothing here of the modern, — from Rome to Babylon, we can point to the existence of Dionysian festivals, types which bear, at best, the same relation to the Greek festivals as the bearded satyr, who borrowed his name and attributes from the goat, does to Dionysus himself. In nearly every case these festivals centered in extravagant sexual licentiousness, whose waves overwhelmed all family life and its venerable traditions; the most savage natural instincts were unleashed, including even that horrible mixture of sensuality and cruelty which has always seemed to me to be the genuine "witches' brew." For some time, however, it would appear that the Greeks were perfectly insulated and guarded against the feverish excitements of these festivals by the figure of Apollo himself rising here in full pride, who could not have held out the Gorgon's head to any power more dangerous than this grotesquely uncouth Dionysian. It is in Doric art that this majestically-rejecting attitude of Apollo is eternized. The opposition between Apollo and Dionysus became more hazardous and even impossible, when, from the deepest roots of the Hellenic nature, similar impulses finally burst forth and made a path for themselves: the Delphic god, by a seasonably effected reconciliation, now contented himself with taking the destructive weapons from the hands of his powerful antagonist. This reconciliation is the most important moment in the history of the Greek cult: wherever we turn we note the revolutions resulting from this event. The two antagonists were reconciled; the boundary lines thenceforth to be observed by each were sharply defined, and there was to be a periodical exchange of gifts of esteem. At bottom, however, the chasm was not bridged over. But if we observe how, under the pressure of this treaty of peace, the Dionysian power revealed itself, we shall now recognize in the Dionysian orgies of the Greeks, as compared with the Babylonian Sacæa with their reversion of man to the tiger and the ape, the significance of festivals of world-redemption and days of transfiguration. It is with them that nature for the first time attains her artistic jubilee; it is with them that the destruction of the *principium individuationis* for the first time becomes an artistic phenomenon. The horrible "witches' brew" of sensuality and cruelty becomes ineffective: only the curious blending and duality in the emotions of the Dionysian revelers remind us — as medicines remind us of deadly poisons — of the phenomenon that pain begets joy, that ecstasy may wring sounds of agony from us. At the very climax of joy there sounds a cry of horror or a yearning lamentation for an irretrievable loss. In these Greek festivals, nature seems to reveal a sentimental trait; it is as if she were heaving a sigh at her dismemberment into individuals. The song and pantomime of such dually-minded revelers was something new and unheard-of for the Homeric-Grecian world: and the Dionysian *music* in particular excited awe and terror. If music, as it would seem, had been known previously as an Apollonian art, it was so, strictly speaking, only as the wave-beat of rhythm, whose formative power was developed for the representation of Apollonian states. The music of Apollo was Doric architectonics in tones, but in tones that were merely suggestive, such as those of the cithara. The very element which forms the essence of Dionysian music (and hence of music in general) is carefully excluded as un-Apollonian: namely, the emotional power of the tone, the uniform flow of the melos, and the utterly incomparable world of harmony. In the Dionysian dithyramb man is incited to the greatest exaltation of all his symbolic faculties; something never before experienced struggles for utterance — the annihilation of the veil of Mâyâ, Oneness as the soul of the race, and of nature itself. The essence of nature is now to be expressed symbolically; we need a new world of symbols; for once the entire symbolism of the body is called into play, not the mere symbolism of the lips, face, and speech, but the whole pantomime of dancing, forcing every member into rhythmic movement. Thereupon the other symbolic powers suddenly press forward, particularly those of music, in rhythmics, dynamics, and harmony. To grasp this collective release of all the symbolic powers, man must have already attained that height of self-abnegation which wills to express itself symbolically through all these powers: and so the dithyrambic votary of Dionysus is understood only by his peers! With what astonishment must the Apollonian Greek have beheld him! With an astonishment that was all the greater the more it was mingled with the shuddering suspicion that all this was actually not so very alien to him after all, in fact, that it was only his Apollonian consciousness which, like a veil, hid this Dionysian world from his vision.

3

TO understand this, it becomes necessary to level the artistic structure of the *Apollonian culture*, as it were, stone by stone, till the foundations on which it rests become visible. First of all we see the glorious *Olympian* figures of the gods, standing on the gables of this structure. Their deeds, pictured in brilliant reliefs, adorn its friezes. We must not be misled by the fact that Apollo stands side by side with the others as an individual deity, without any claim to priority of rank. For the same impulse which embodied itself in Apollo gave birth in general to this entire Olympian world, and so in this sense Apollo is its father. What terrific need was it that could produce such an illustrious company of Olympian beings?

He who approaches these Olympians with another religion in his heart, seeking among them for moral elevation, even for sanctity, for disincarnate spirituality, for charity and benevolence, will soon be forced to turn his back on them, discouraged and disappointed. For there is nothing here that suggests asceticism, spirituality, or duty. We hear nothing but the accents of an exuberant, triumphant life, in which all things, whether good or bad, are deified. And so the spectator may stand quite bewildered before this fantastic superfluity of life, asking himself what magic potion these mad glad men could have imbibed to make life so enjoyable that, wherever they turned, their eyes beheld the smile of Helen, the ideal picture of their own existence, "floating in sweet sensuality." But to this spectator, who has his back already turned, we must perforce cry: "Go not away, but stay and hear what Greek folk-wisdom has to say of this very life, which with such inexplicable gayety unfolds itself before your eyes. There is an ancient story that King Midas hunted in the forest a long time for the wise *Silenus*, the companion of Dionysus, without capturing him. When Silenus at last fell into his hands, the king asked what was the best and most desirable of all things for man. Fixed and immovable, the demigod said not a word; till at last, urged by the king, he gave a shrill laugh and broke out into these words: 'Oh, wretched ephemeral race, children of chance and misery, why do ye compel me to tell you what it were most expedient for you not to hear? What is best of all is beyond your reach forever: not to be born, not to *be*, to be *nothing*. But the second best for you — is quickly to die.' "

How is the Olympian world of deities related to this folk-wisdom? Even as the rapturous vision of the tortured martyr to his suffering.

Now it is as if the Olympian magic mountain had opened before us and revealed its roots to us. The Greek knew and felt the terror and horror of existence. That he might endure this terror at all, he had to interpose between himself and life the radiant dream-birth of the Olympians. That overwhelming dismay in the face of the titanic powers of nature, the Moira enthroned inexorably over all knowledge, the vulture of the great lover of mankind, Prometheus, the terrible fate of the wise Œdipus, the family curse of the Atridæ which drove Orestes to matricide: in short, that entire philosophy of the sylvan god, with its mythical exemplars, which caused the downfall of the melancholy Etruscans — all this was again and again overcome by the Greeks with the aid of the Olympian *middle world* of art; or at any rate it was veiled and withdrawn from sight. It was out of the direst necessity to live that the Greeks created these gods. Perhaps we may picture the process to ourselves somewhat as follows: out of the original Titan thearchy of terror the Olympian thearchy of joy gradually evolved through the Apollonian impulse towards beauty, just as roses bud from thorny bushes. How else could this people, so sensitive, so vehement in its desires, so singularly constituted for *suffering*, how could they have endured existence, if it had not been revealed to them in their gods, surrounded with a higher glory? The same impulse which calls art into being, as the complement and consummation of existence, seducing one to a continuation of life, was also the cause of the Olympian world which the Hellenic "will" made use of as a transfiguring mirror. Thus do the gods justify the life of man, in that they themselves live it — the only satisfactory Theodicy! Existence under the bright sunshine of such gods is regarded as desirable in itself, and the real *grief* of the Homeric men is caused by parting from it, especially by early parting: so that now, reversing the wisdom of Silenus, we might say of the Greeks that "to die early is worst of all for them, the next worst — some day to die at all." Once heard, it will ring out again; forget not the lament of the short-lived Achilles, mourning the leaflike change and vicissitude of the race of men and the decline of the heroic age. It is not unworthy of the greatest hero to long for a continuation of life, aye, even though he live as a slave. At the Apollonian stage of development, the "will" longs so vehemently for this existence, the Homeric man feels himself so completely at one with it, that lamentation itself becomes a song of praise.

Here we should note that this harmony which is contemplated with such longing by modern man, in fact, this oneness of man with nature (to express which Schiller introduced the technical term "naïve"), is by no means a simple condition, resulting naturally, and as if inevitably. It is not a condition which, like a terrestrial paradise, *must* necessarily be found at the gate of every culture. Only a romantic age could believe this, an age which conceived of the artist in terms of Rousseau's *Emile* and imagined that in Homer it had found such an artist Emile, reared in Nature's bosom. Wherever we meet with the "naïve" in art, we recognize the highest effect of the Apollonian culture, which in the first place has always to overthrow some Titanic empire and slay monsters, and which, through its potent dazzling representations and its pleasurable illusions, must have triumphed over a terrible depth of world-contemplation and a most keen sensitivity to suffering. But how seldom do we attain to the naïve — that complete absorption in the beauty of appearance! And hence how inexpressibly sublime is *Homer*, who, as individual being, bears the same relation to this Apollonian folk-culture as the individual dream-artist does to the dream-faculty of the people and of Nature in general. The Homeric "naïveté" can be understood only as the complete victory of the Apollonian illusion: an illusion similar to those which Nature so frequently employs to achieve her own ends. The true goal is veiled by a phantasm: and while we stretch out our hands for the latter, Nature attains the former by means of your illusion. In the Greeks the "will" wished to contemplate itself in the transfiguration of genius and the world of art; in order to glorify themselves, its creatures had to feel themselves worthy of glory; they had to behold themselves again in a higher sphere, without this perfect world of contemplation acting as a command or a reproach. Such is the sphere of beauty, in which they saw their mirrored images, the Olympians. With this mirroring of beauty the Hellenic will combated its artistically correlative talent for suffering and for the wisdom of suffering: and, as a monument of its victory, we have Homer, the naïve artist.

4

NOW the dream-analogy may throw some light on the problem of the naïve artist. Let us imagine the dreamer: in the midst of the illusion of the dream-world and without disturbing it, he calls out to himself: "It is a dream, I will dream on." What must we infer? That he experiences a deep inner joy in dream-contemplation; on the other hand, to be at all able to dream with this inner joy in contemplation, he must have completely lost sight of the waking reality and its ominous obtrusiveness. Guided by the dream-reading Apollo, we may interpret all these phenomena to ourselves somewhat in this way. Though it is certain that of the two halves of our existence, the waking and the dreaming states, the former appeals to us as infinitely preferable, important, excellent and worthy of being lived, indeed, as that which alone is lived: yet, in relation to that mysterious substratum of our nature of which we are the phenomena, I should, paradoxical as it may seem, maintain the very opposite estimate of the value of dream life. For the more clearly I perceive in Nature those omnipotent art impulses, and in them an ardent longing for release, for redemption through release, the more I feel myself impelled to the metaphysical assumption that the Truly-Existent and Primal Unity, eternally suffering and divided against itself, has need of the rapturous vision, the joyful appearance, for its continuous salvation: which appearance we, completely wrapped up in it and composed of it, are compelled to apprehend as the True Non-Being, — *i.e.*, as a perpetual becoming in time, space and causality, — in other words, as empiric reality. If, for the moment, we do not consider the question of our own "reality," if we conceive of our empirical existence, and that of the world in general, as a continuously manifested representation of the Primal Unity, we shall then have to look upon the dream as an *appearance of appearance*, hence as a still higher appeasement of the primordial desire for appearance. And that is why the innermost heart of Nature feels that ineffable joy in the naïve artist and the naïve work of art, which is likewise only "an appearance of appearance." In a symbolic painting, *Raphael*, himself one of these immortal "naïve" ones, has represented for us this devolution of appearance to appearance, the primitive process of the naïve artist and of Apollonian culture. In his "Trans-figuration," the lower half of the picture, with the possessed boy, the despairing bearers, the bewildered, terrified disciples, shows us the reflection of suffering, primal and eternal, the sole basis of the world: the "appearance" here is the counter-appearance of eternal contradic-tion, the father of things. From this appearance now arises, like ambro-sial vapor, a new visionary world of appearances, invisible to those wrapped in the first appearance — a radiant floating in purest bliss, a serene contemplation beaming from wide-open eyes. Here we have presented, in the most sublime artistic symbolism, that Apollonian world of beauty and its substratum, the terrible wisdom of Silenus; and intuitively we comprehend their necessary interdependence. Apollo, however, again appears to us as the apotheosis of the *principium individuationis*, in which alone is consummated the perpetually at-tained goal of the Primal Unity, its redemption through appearance. With his sublime gestures, he shows us how necessary is the entire world of suffering, that by means of it the individual may be impelled to realize the redeeming vision, and then, sunk in contemplation of it, sit quietly in his tossing barque, amid the waves.

If we at all conceive of it as imperative and mandatory, this apotheosis of individuation knows but one law — the individual, *i.e.*, the delimiting of the boundaries of the individual, *measure* in the Hellenic sense. Apollo, as ethical deity, exacts measure of his disciples, and, that to this end, he requires self-knowledge. And so, side by side with the esthetic necessity for beauty, there occur the demands "know thyself" and "noth-ing overmuch"; consequently pride and excess are regarded as the truly inimical demons of the non-Apollonian sphere, hence as characteristics of the pre-Apollonian age — that of the Titans; and of the extra-Apollonian world — that of the barbarians. Because of his Titan-like love for man, Prometheus must be torn to pieces by vultures; because of his excessive wisdom, which could solve the riddle of the Sphinx, Œdipus must be plunged into a bewildering vortex of crime. Thus did the Delphic god interpret the Greek past.

Similarly the effects wrought by the *Dionysian* seemed "titan-like" and "barbaric" to the Apollonian Greek: while at the same time he could not conceal from himself that he too was inwardly related to these overthrown Titans and heroes. Indeed, he had to recognize even more than this: despite all its beauty and moderation, his entire existence rested on a hidden substratum of suffering and of knowledge, which was again revealed to him by the Dionysian. And lo! Apollo could not live without Dionysus! The "titanic" and the "barbaric" were in the last analysis as necessary as the Apollonian.

And now let us take this artistically limited world, based on appearance and moderation; let us imagine how into it there penetrated, in tones ever more bewitching and alluring, the ecstatic sound of the Dionysian festival; let us remember that in these strains all of Nature's excess in joy, sorrow, and knowledge become audible, even in piercing shrieks; and finally, let us ask ourselves what significance remains to the psalmodizing artist of Apollo, with his phantom harp-sound, once it is compared with this demonic folk-song! The muses of the arts of "appearance" paled before an art which, in its intoxication, spoke the truth. The wisdom of Silenus cried "Woe! woe!" to the serene Olympians. The individual, with all his restraint and proportion, succumbed to the self-oblivion of the Dionysian state, forgetting the precepts of Apollo. Excess revealed itself as truth. Contradiction, the bliss born of pain, spoke out from the very heart of Nature. And so, wherever the Dionysian prevailed, the Apollonian was checked and destroyed. But, on the other hand, it is equally certain that, wherever the first Dionysian onslaught was successfully withstood, the authority and majesty of the Delphic god exhibited itself as more rigid and menacing than ever. For to me the *Doric* state and Doric art are explicable only as a permanent citadel of the Apollonian. For an art so defiantly prim, and so encompassed with bulwarks, a training so warlike and rigorous, a political structure so cruel and relentless, could endure for any length of time only by incessant opposition to the titanic-barbaric nature of the Dionysian.

Up to this point we have simply enlarged upon the observation made at the beginning of this essay: that the Dionysian and the Apollonian, in new births ever following and mutually augmenting one another, controlled the Hellenic genius; that from out the age of "bronze," with its wars of the Titans and its rigorous folk-philosophy, the Homeric world developed under the sway of the Apollonian impulse to beauty; that this "naïve" splendor was again overwhelmed by the influx of the Dionysian; and that against this new power the Apollonian rose to the austere majesty of Doric art and the Doric view of the world. If, then, amid the strife of these two hostile principles, the older Hellenic history thus falls into four great periods of art, we are now impelled to inquire after the *final goal* of these developments and processes, lest perchance we should regard the last-attained period, the period of Doric art, as the climax and aim of these artistic impulses. And here the sublime and celebrated art of *Attic tragedy* and the dramatic dithyramb presents itself as the common goal of both these tendencies, whose mysterious union, after many and long precursory struggles, found glorious consummation in this child, — at once Antigone and Cassandra.

5

WE now approach the real goal of our investigation, which is directed towards acquiring a knowledge of the Dionysian-Apollonian genius and its art-product, or at least an anticipatory understanding of its mysterious union. Here we shall first of all inquire after the first evidence in Greece of that new germ which subsequently developed into tragedy and the dramatic dithyramb. The ancients themselves give us a symbolic answer, when they place the faces of *Homer* and *Archilochus* as the forefathers and torchbearers of Greek poetry side by side on gems, sculptures, etc., with a sure feeling that consideration should be given only to these two thoroughly original compeers, from whom a stream of fire flows over the whole of later Greek history. Homer, the aged self-absorbed dreamer, the type of the Apollonian naïve artist, now beholds with astonishment the passionate genius of the war-like votary of the muses, Archilochus, passing through life with fury and violence; and modern esthetics, by way of interpretation, can only add that here the first "objective" artist confronts the first "subjective" artist. But this interpretation helps us but little, because we know the subjective artist only as the poor artist, and throughout the entire range of art we demand specially and first of all the conquest of the Subjective, the release from the ego and the silencing of the individual will and desire; indeed, we find it impossible to believe in any truly artistic production, however insignificant, if it is without objectivity, without pure, detached contemplation. Hence our esthetic must first solve the problem of how the "lyrist" is possible as an artist — he who, according to the experience of all ages, is continually saying "I" and running through the entire chromatic scale of his passions and desires. Compared with Homer, this very Archilochus appalls us by his cries of hatred and scorn, by his drunken outbursts of desire. Therefore is not he, who has been called the first subjective artist, essentially the non-artist? But in this case, how explain the reverence which was shown to him — the poet — in very remarkable utterances by the Delphic oracle itself, the center of "objective" art?

Schiller has thrown some light on the poetic process by a psychological observation, inexplicable to himself, yet apparently valid. He admits that before the act of creation he did not perhaps have before him or within him any series of images accompanied by an ordered thought-relationship; but his condition was rather that of a *musical mood.* ("With me the perception has at first no clear and definite object; this is formed later. A certain musical mood of mind precedes, and only after this ensues the poetical idea.") Let us add to this the natural and most important phenomenon of all ancient lyric poetry, *the union,* indeed, the *identity,* of the *lyrist with the musician,* — compared with which our modern lyric poetry appears like the statue of a god without a head, — with this in mind we may now, on the basis of our metaphysics of esthetics set forth above, explain the lyrist to ourselves in this manner: In the first place, as Dionysian artist he has identified himself with the Primal Unity, its pain and contradiction. Assuming that music has been correctly termed a repetition and a recast of the world, we may say that he produces the copy of this Primal Unity as music. Now, however, under the Apollonian dream-inspiration, this music reveals itself to him again as a *symbolic dream-picture.* The inchoate, intangible reflection of the primordial pain in music, with its redemption in appearance, now produces a second mirroring as a specific symbol or example. The artist has already surrendered his subjectivity in the Dionysian process. The picture which now shows him his identity with the heart of the world, is a dream-scene, which embodies the primordial contradiction and primordial pain, together with the primordial joy, of appearance. The "I" of the lyrist therefore sounds from the depth of his being: its "subjectivity," in the sense of the modern esthetes, is pure imagination. When Archilochus, the first Greek lyrist, proclaims to the daughters of Lycambes both his mad love and his contempt, it is not his passion alone which dances before us in orgiastic frenzy; but we see Dionysus and the Mænads, we see the drunken reveler Archilochus sunk down in slumber — as Euripides depicts it in the *Bacchæ,* the sleep on the high mountain pasture, in the noonday sun. And now Apollo approaches and touches him with the laurel. Then the Dionyso-musical enchantment of the sleeper seems to emit picture sparks, lyrical poems, which in their highest form are called tragedies and dramatic dithyrambs.

The plastic artist, as also the epic poet, who is related to him, is sunk in the pure contemplation of images. The Dionysian musician is, without any images, himself pure primordial pain and its primordial reëchoing. The lyric genius is conscious of a world of pictures and symbols — growing out of his state of mystical self-abnegation and oneness. This state has a coloring, a causality and a velocity quite different from that of the world of the plastic artist and the epic poet. For the latter lives in these pictures, and only in them, with joyful satisfaction. He never grows tired of contemplating lovingly even their minutest traits. Even the picture of the angry Achilles is only a picture to him, whose angry expression he enjoys with the dream-joy in appearance. Thus, by this mirror of appearance, he is protected against being united and blended with his figures. In direct contrast to this, the pictures of the *lyrist* are nothing but *his very* self and, as it were, only different projections of himself, by force of which he, as the moving center of this world, may say "I": only of course this self is not the same as that of the waking, empirically real man, but the only truly existent and eternal self resting at the basis of things, and with the help of whose images, the lyric genius can penetrate to this very basis.

Now let us suppose that among these images he also beholds *himself* as non-genius, *i.e.*, his subject, the whole throng of subjective passions and agitations directed to a definite object which appears real to him. It may now seem as if the lyric genius and the allied non-genius were one, as if the former had of its own accord spoken that little word "I." But this identity is but superficial and it will no longer be able to lead us astray, as it certainly led astray those who designated the lyrist as the subjective poet. For, as a matter of fact, Archilochus, the passionately inflamed, loving and hating man, is but a vision of the genius, who by this time is no longer merely Archilochus, but a world-genius expressing his primordial pain symbolically in the likeness of the man Archilochus: while the subjectively willing and desiring man, Archilochus, can never at any time be a poet. It is by no means necessary, however, that the lyrist should see nothing but the phenomenon of the man Archilochus before him as a reflection of eternal being; and tragedy shows how far the visionary world of the lyrist may be removed from this phenomenon, which, of course, is intimately related to it.

Schopenhauer, who did not conceal from himself the difficulty the lyrist presents in the philosophical contemplation of art, thought he had found a solution, with which, however, I am not in entire accord. (Actually, it was in his profound metaphysics of music that he alone held in his hands the means whereby this difficulty might be definitely removed: as I believe I have removed it here in his spirit and to his honor). In contrast to our view, he describes the peculiar nature of song as follows[3] (*Welt als Wille und Vorstellung*, I. 295):

"It is the subject of will, *i.e.*, his own volition, which the consciousness of the singer feels; often as a released and satisfied desire (joy), but still oftener as a restricted desire (grief), always as an emotion, a passion, a moved frame of mind. Besides this, however, and along with it, by the sight of surrounding nature, the singer becomes conscious of himself as the subject of pure will-less knowing, whose unbroken, blissful peace now appears, in contrast to the stress of desire, which is always restricted and always needy. The feeling of this contrast, this alternation, is really what the lyric as a whole expresses and what principally constitutes the lyrical state of mind. In it pure knowing comes to us as it were to deliver us from desire and its strain; we follow, but only for an instant; desire, the remembrance of our own personal ends, tears us anew from peaceful contemplation; yet ever again the next beautiful surrounding in which the pure will-less knowledge presents itself to us, allures us away from desire. Therefore, in the lyric and the lyrical mood, desire (the personal interest of the ends) and pure perception of the surrounding presented are wonderfully mingled with each other; connections between them are sought for and imagined; the subjective disposition, the affection of the will, imparts its own hue to the perceived surrounding, and conversely, the surroundings communicate the reflex of their color to the will. The true lyric is the expression of the whole of this mingled and divided state of mind."

Who could fail to recognize in this description that lyric poetry is here characterized as an incompletely attained art, which arrives at its goal infrequently and only as it were by leaps? Indeed, it is described as a semi-art, whose essence is said to consist in this, that desire and pure contemplation, *i.e.*, the unesthetic and the esthetic condition, are wonderfully mingled with each other. It follows that Schopenhauer still classifies the arts as subjective or objective, using the antithesis as if it were a criterion of value. But it is our contention, on the contrary, that this antithesis between the subjective and the objective is especially irrelevant in esthetics, since the subject, the desiring individual furthering his own egoistic ends, can be conceived of only as the antagonist, not as the origin of art. In so far as the subject is the artist, however, he has already been released from his individual will, and has become as it were the medium through which the one truly existent Subject celebrates his release in appearance. For, above all, to our humiliation *and*

---

[3] *World as Will and Idea*, I. 322, trans. by Haldane and Kemp, 6th ed.

exaltation, one thing must be clear to us. The entire comedy of art is neither performed for our betterment or education nor are we the true authors of this art-world. On the contrary, we may assume that we are merely pictures and artistic projections for the true author, and that we have our highest dignity in our significance as works of art — for it is only as an *esthetic phenomenon* that existence and the world are eternally *justified* — while of course our consciousness of our own significance hardly differs from that which the soldiers painted on canvas have of the battle represented on it. Thus all our knowledge of art is basically quite illusory, because as knowing beings we are not one and identical with that Being who, as the sole author and spectator of this comedy of art, prepares a perpetual entertainment for himself. Only in so far as the genius in the act of artistic creation coalesces with this primordial artist of the world, does he catch sight of the eternal essence of art; for in this state he is, in a marvelous manner, like the weird picture of the fairy-tale which can turn its eyes at will and behold itself; he is now at once subject and object, at once poet, actor, and spectator.

6

IN connection with Archilochus, scholarly research has discovered that he introduced the *folk-song* into literature, and, on account of this, deserved, according to the general estimate of the Greeks, his unique position beside Homer. But what is the folk-song in contrast to the wholly Apollonian epos? What else but the *perpetuum vestigium* of a union of the Apollonian and the Dionysian? Its enormous diffusion among all peoples, further re-enforced by ever-new births, is testimony to the power of this artistic dual impulse of Nature: which leaves its vestiges in the folk-song just as the orgiastic movements of a people perpetuate themselves in its music. Indeed, it might also be historically demonstrable that every period rich in folk-songs has been most violently stirred by Dionysian currents, which we must always consider the substratum and prerequisite of the folk-song.

First of all, however, we must conceive the folk-song as the musical mirror of the world, as the original melody, now seeking for itself a parallel dream-phenomenon and expressing it in poetry. *Melody is therefore primary and universal*, and so may admit of several objectifications in several texts. Likewise, in the naïve estimation of the people, it is regarded as by far the more important and essential element. Melody generates the poem out of itself by a continuous process. *The strophic form of the folk-song* points to the same thing; a phenomenon which I had always beheld with astonishment, until at last I found this explanation. Any one who in accordance with this theory examines a collection of folk-songs, such as *Des Knaben Wunderhorn*, will find innumerable instances of the way the continuously generating melody scatters picture sparks all around, which in their variegation, their abrupt change, their mad precipitation, manifest a power quite unknown to the epic and its steady flow. From the standpoint of the epos, this unequal and irregular pictorial world of lyric poetry is definitely to be condemned: and it certainly has been thus condemned by the solemn epic rhapsodists of the Apollonian festivals in the age of Terpander.

Accordingly, we observe that in the poetry of the folk-song, language is strained to its utmost that it may *imitate music;* and hence with Archilochus begins a new world of poetry, which is basically opposed to the Homeric. And in saying this we have indicated the only possible relation between poetry and music, between word and tone: the word, the picture, the concept here seeks an expression analogous to music and now feels in itself the power of music. In this sense we may discriminate between two main currents in the history of the language of the Greek people, according to whether their language imitated the world of image and phenomenon, or the world of music. One need only reflect more deeply on the linguistic difference with regard to color, syntactical structure, and vocabulary in Homer and Pindar, in order to understand the significance of this contrast; indeed, it becomes palpably clear that in the period between Homer and Pindar there must have sounded out the *orgiastic flute tones of Olympus*, which, even in Aristotle's time, when music was infinitely more developed, transported people to drunken ecstasy, and which, in their primitive state of development, undoubtedly incited to imitation all the poetic means of expression of contemporaneous man. I here call attention to a familiar phenomenon of our own times, against which our esthetic raises many objections. We again and again have occasion to observe that a Beethoven symphony compels its individual auditors to use figurative speech in describing it, no matter how fantastically variegated and even contradictory may be the composition and make-up of the different pictorial world produced by a piece of music. To exercise its poor wit on such compositions, and to overlook a phenomenon which is certainly worth explaining, is quite in keeping with this esthetic. Indeed, even when the tone-poet expresses his composition in pictures, when for instance he designates a certain symphony as the "pastoral" symphony, or a passage in it as the "scene by the brook," or another as the "merry gathering of rustics," these too are only symbolical representations born of music — and not perhaps the imitated objects of music — representations which can teach us nothing whatsoever concerning the *Dionysian* content of music, and which indeed have no distinctive value of their own beside other pictorial expressions. We have now to transfer this process of a discharge of music in pictures to some fresh, youthful, linguistically creative people, in order to get a notion of how the strophic faculty of speech is stimulated by this new principle of the imitation of music.

If, therefore, we may regard lyric poetry as the fulguration of music in images and concepts, we should now ask: "In what form does music *appear* in the mirror of symbolism and conception?" *It appears as will*, taking the term in Schopenhauer's sense, *i.e.*, as the antithesis of the esthetic, purely contemplative, and passive frame of mind. Here, however, we must make as sharp a distinction as possible between the concept of essence and the concept of phenomenon; for music, according to its essence, cannot possibly be will. To be will it would have to be wholly banished from the realm of art — for the will is the unesthetic-in-itself. Yet though *essentially* it is not will, *phenomenally* it *appears* as will. For in order to express the phenomenon of music in images, the lyrist needs all the agitations of passion, from the whisper of mere inclination to the roar of madness. Impelled to speak of music in Apollonian symbols, he conceives of all nature, and himself therein, only as eternal Will, Desire, Longing. But in so far as he interprets music by means of images, he himself rests in the quiet calm of Apollonian contemplation, though everything around him which he beholds through the medium of music may be confused and violent. Indeed, when he beholds himself through this same medium, his own image appears to him as an unsatisfied feeling: his own willing, longing, moaning, rejoicing, are to him symbols by which he interprets music. This is the phenomenon of the lyrist: as Apollonian genius he interprets music through the image of the will, while he himself, completely released from the desire of the will, is the pure, undimmed eye of day.

Our whole discussion insists that lyric poetry is dependent on the spirit of music just as music itself in its absolute sovereignty does not need the picture and the concept, but merely *endures* them as accompaniments. The poems of the lyrist can express nothing which did not already lie hidden in the vast universality and absoluteness of the music which compelled him to figurative speech. Language can never adequately render the cosmic symbolism of music, because music stands in symbolic relation to the primordial contradiction and primordial pain in the heart of the Primal Unity, and therefore symbolizes a sphere which is beyond and before all phenomena. Rather are all phenomena, compared with it, merely symbols: hence *language*, as the organ and symbol of phenomena, can never, by any means, disclose the innermost heart of music; language, in its attempt to imitate it, can only be in superficial contact with music; while the deepest significance of the latter cannot with all the eloquence of lyric poetry be brought one step nearer to us.

7

WE must now avail ourselves of all the principles of art hitherto considered, in order to find our way through the labyrinth, as we must call it, of *the origin of Greek tragedy*. I do not think I am unreasonable in saying that the problem of this origin has as yet not even been seriously stated, not to say solved, however often the ragged tatters of ancient tradition are sewn together in various combinations and torn apart again. This tradition tells us quite unequivocally, *that tragedy arose from the tragic chorus*, and was originally only chorus and nothing but chorus; and hence we feel it our duty to look into the heart of this tragic chorus as being the real proto-drama. We shall not let ourselves be at all satisfied with that current art-lingo which makes the chorus the "ideal spectator," or has it represent the people in contrast to the aristocratic elements of the scene. This latter explanation has a sublime sound to many a politician. It insists that the immutable moral law was embodied by the democratic Athenians in the popular chorus, which always wins out over the passionate excesses and extravagances of kings. This theory may be ever so forcibly suggested by one of Aristotle's observations; still, it has no influence on the original formation of tragedy, inasmuch as the entire antithesis of king and people, and, in general, the whole politico-social sphere, is excluded from the purely religious origins of tragedy. With this in mind, and remembering the well-known classical form of the chorus in Æschylus and Sophocles, we should even deem it blasphemy to speak here of the anticipation of a "constitutional popular representation." From this blasphemy, however, others have not shrunk. The ancient governments knew of no constitutional representation of the people *in praxi*, and it is to be hoped that they did not "anticipate" it in their tragedy either.

Much more famous than this political interpretation of the chorus is the theory of A. W. Schlegel, who advises us to regard the chorus, in a manner, as the essence and extract of the crowd of spectators, — as the "ideal spectator." This view, when compared with the historical tradition that originally tragedy was only chorus, reveals itself for what it is, — a crude, unscientific, yet brilliant generalization, which, however, acquires that brilliancy only through its epigrammatic form of expression, the deep Germanic bias in favor of anything called "ideal," and our momentary astonishment. For we are certainly astonished the moment we compare our familiar theatrical public with this chorus, and ask ourselves whether it could ever be possible to idealize something analogous to the Greek tragic chorus out of such a public. We tacitly deny this, and now wonder as much at the boldness of Schlegel's assertion as at the totally different nature of the Greek public. For hitherto we had always believed that the true spectator, whoever he may be, must always remain conscious that he was viewing a work of art, and not an empirical reality. But the tragic chorus of the Greeks is forced to recognize *real beings* in the figures of the drama. The chorus of the Oceanides really believes that it sees before it the Titan Prometheus, and considers itself as real as the god of the scene. And are we to designate as the highest and purest type of spectator, one who, like the Oceanides, regards Prometheus as real and present in body? Is it characteristic of the ideal spectator to run on to the stage and free the god from his torments? We had always believed in an esthetic public, we had considered the individual spectator the better qualified the more he was capable of viewing a work of art as art, that is, esthetically. But now Schlegel tells us that the perfect ideal spectator does not at all allow the world of the drama to act on him *esthetically*, but corporeally and empirically. Oh, these Greeks! we sighed; they upset all our esthetics! . . . But once accustomed to it, we have repeated Schlegel's saying whenever the chorus came up for discussion.

Now, the tradition which is quite explicit here, speaks against Schlegel. The chorus as such, without the stage, — the primitive form of tragedy, — and the chorus of ideal spectators do not go together. What kind of art would that be in which the spectator does not enter as a separate concept? What kind of art is that whose true form is identical with the "spectator as such"? The spectator without the play is nonsense. We fear that the birth of tragedy is to be explained neither by the high esteem for the moral intelligence of the multitude nor by the concept of the spectator minus the play. We must regard the problem as too deep to be even touched by such superficial generalizing.

An infinitely more valuable insight into the significance of the chorus had already been displayed by Schiller in the celebrated Preface to his *Bride of Messina*, where he regards the chorus as a living barrier which tragedy constructs round herself to cut off her contact with the world of reality, and to preserve her ideal domain and her poetical freedom.

With this, his chief weapon, Schiller combats the ordinary conception of the natural, the illusion usually demanded in dramatic poetry. Although it is true that the stage day is merely artificial, the architecture only symbolical, and the metrical language purely ideal in character, nevertheless an erroneous view still prevails in the main: that we should not excuse these conventions merely on the ground that they constitute a poetical license. Now in reality these "conventions" form the essence of all poetry. The introduction of the chorus, says Schiller, is the decisive step by which open and honorable war is declared against all naturalism in art. It would seem that to denigrate this view of the matter our would-be superior age has coined the disdainful catchword "pseudo-idealism." I fear, however, that we, on the other hand, with our present adoration of the natural and the real, have reached the opposite pole of all idealism, namely, in the region of wax-work cabinets. There is an art in these too, as certain novels much in vogue at present evidence: but let us not disturb ourselves at the claim that by any such art the Schiller-Goethian "pseudo-idealism" has been vanquished.

It is indeed an "ideal" domain, as Schiller correctly perceived, in which the Greek satyr chorus, the chorus of primitive tragedy, was wont to dwell. It is a domain raised high above the actual path of mortals. For this chorus the Greek built up the scaffolding of a fictitious *natural state* and on it placed fictitious *natural beings*. On this foundation tragedy developed and so, of course, it could dispense from the beginning with a painful portrayal of reality. Yet it is no arbitrary world placed by whim between heaven and earth; rather is it a world with the same reality and credibility that Olympus with its dwellers possessed for the believing Hellene. The satyr, as the Dionysian chorist, lives in a religiously acknowledged reality under the sanction of the myth and the cult. That tragedy should begin with him, that he should be the voice of the Dionysian tragic wisdom, is just as strange a phenomenon as the general derivation of tragedy from the chorus.

Perhaps we shall have a point of departure for our inquiry, if I put forward the proposition that the satyr, the fictitious natural being, bears the same relation to the man of culture that Dionysian music does to civilization. Concerning this latter, Richard Wagner says that it is neutralized by music just as lamplight is neutralized by the light of day. Similarly, I believe, the Greek man of culture felt himself neutralized in the presence of the satyric chorus: and this is the most immediate effect of the Dionysian tragedy, that the state and society, and, in general, the gulfs between man and man give way to an overwhelming feeling of unity leading back to the very heart of nature. The metaphysical comfort — with which, as I have here intimated, every true tragedy leaves us — that, in spite of the flux of phenomena, life at bottom is indestructibly powerful and pleasurable, appears with objective clarity as the satyr chorus, the chorus of natural beings, who as it were live ineradicably behind every civilization, and who, despite the ceaseless change of generations and the history of nations, remain the same to all eternity.

With this chorus the deep-minded Hellene consoles himself, he who is so singularly constituted for the most sensitive and grievous suffering, he who with a piercing glance has penetrated into the very heart of the terrible destructive processes of so-called universal history, as also into the cruelty of nature, and who is in danger of longing for a Buddhistic negation of the will. Art saves him, and through art life saves him — for herself.

For we must realize that in the ecstasy of the Dionysian state, with its annihilation of the ordinary bounds and limits of existence, there is contained a *lethargic* element, in which are submerged all past personal experiences. It is this gulf of oblivion that separates the world of everyday from the world of Dionysian reality. But as soon as we become conscious again of this everyday reality, we feel it as nauseating and repulsive; and an ascetic will-negating mood is the fruit of these states. In this sense the Dionysian man resembles Hamlet: both have for once penetrated into the true nature of things, — they have *perceived*, but it is irksome for them to act; for their action cannot change the eternal nature of things; the time is out of joint and they regard it as shameful or ridiculous that they should be required to set it right. Knowledge kills action, action requires the veil of illusion — it is this lesson which Hamlet teaches, and not the idle wisdom of John-o'-Dreams who from too much reflection, from a surplus of possibilities, never arrives at action at all. Not reflection, no! — true knowledge, insight into the terrible truth, preponderate over all motives inciting to action, in Hamlet as well as in the Dionysian man. There is no longer any use in comfort; his longing goes beyond a world after death, beyond the gods themselves; existence with its glittering reflection in the gods or in an immortal beyond is abjured. In the consciousness of the truth once perceived, man now sees everywhere only the terror or the absurdity of existence; now he can understand the symbolism of Ophelia's fate; now he can realize the wisdom of the sylvan god Silenus: and he is filled with loathing.

But at this juncture, when the will is most imperiled, *art* approaches, as a redeeming and healing enchantress; she alone may transform these horrible reflections on the terror and absurdity of existence into representations with which man may live. These are the representation of the *sublime* as the artistic conquest of the awful, and of the *comic* as the artistic release from the nausea of the absurd. The satyric chorus of the dithyramb is the saving device of Greek art; the paroxysms described above exhaust themselves in the intermediary world of these Dionysian votaries.

8

THE satyr, like the idyllic shepherd of our more recent time, is the offspring of a longing for the Primitive and the Natural; but how firmly and fearlessly the Greek embraced the man of the woods, and how timorously and mawkishly modern man dallied with the flattering picture of a sentimental, flute-playing, soft-mannered shepherd! Nature, as yet unchanged by knowledge, maintaining impregnable barriers to culture — that is what the Greek saw in his satyr, which nevertheless was not on this account to be confused with the primitive cave-man. On the contrary, the satyr was the archetype of man, the embodiment of his highest and intensest emotions, the ecstatic reveler enraptured by the proximity of his god, the sympathetic companion in whom is repeated the suffering of the god, wisdom's harbinger speaking from the very heart of nature, emblem of the sexual omnipotence of nature, which the Greek was wont to contemplate with reverence and wonder. The satyr was something sublime and godlike: it was inevitable that he should appear so, especially to the sad downcast glance of the Dionysian man. Our counterfeit tricked-up shepherd would have repulsed the Dionysian; but on the naked and magnificent characters of nature his eye dwelt with rapt satisfaction. Here the illusion of culture was cast off from the archetype of man; here the true man, the bearded satyr, revealed himself, shouting joyfully to his god. Face to face with him the man of culture shrank to a specious caricature. Schiller is right also with regard to these beginnings of tragic art: the chorus is a living bulwark against the onslaught of reality, because it — the satyr chorus — portrays existence more truthfully, more essentially, more perfectly than the cultured man who ordinarily considers himself as the sole reality. The sphere of poetry does not lie outside the world, like some chimera of the poetic imagination; it seeks to be the very opposite, the unvarnished expression of truth, and for this very reason it must reject the false finery of that supposed reality of the cultured man. The contrast between this intrinsic truth of nature and the falsehood of culture, which poses as the only reality, is similar to that existing between the eternal heart of things, the thing in itself, and the collective world of phenomena. And just as tragedy, with its metaphysical comfort, points to the eternal life of this kernel of existence, and to the perpetual dissolution of phenomena, so the symbolism of the satyr chorus already expresses figuratively this primal relation between the thing in itself and the phenomenon. The idyllic shepherd of the modern man is but a copy of the sum of the culture — illusions which he calls nature; the Dionysian Greek desires truth and nature in their most potent form — and so he sees himself metamorphosed into the satyr.

The reveling throng of the votaries of Dionysus rejoice under the influence of such moods and perceptions, the power of which transforms them before their own eyes, so that they imagine they behold themselves as recreated genii of nature, as satyrs. The latter constitution of the tragic chorus is the artistic imitation of this natural phenomenon, which of course necessitated a separation of the Dionysian spectators from the enchanted Dionysians. However, we must always remember that the public of the Attic tragedy rediscovered itself in the chorus of the orchestra, that there was at bottom no opposition of public and chorus: for all was but one great sublime chorus of dancing and singing satyrs, or of such as allowed themselves to be represented by these satyrs. Schlegel's observation in this sense reveals a deeper significance. The chorus *is* the "ideal spectator"[4] in so far as it is the only *beholder*,[5] the beholder of the visionary world of the scene. A public of spectators, as we know it, was unknown to the Greeks. In their theaters the terraced structure of the theatron rising in concentric arcs enabled every one to *overlook*, in an actual sense, the entire world of culture around him, and in an over-abundance of contemplation to imagine himself one of the chorus. According to this view, then, we may call the chorus in its primitive stage in early tragedy a self-mirroring of the Dionysian man: a phenomenon which is most clearly exemplified by the process of the actor, who, if he be truly gifted, sees hovering almost tangibly before his eyes the character he is to represent. The satyr chorus is above all a vision of the Dionysian throng, just as the world of the stage is, in turn, a vision of the satyr chorus. The power of this vision is great enough to render the eye dull and insensible to the impression of "reality," to the presence of the cultured men occupying the tiers of seats on every side. The form of the Greek theater reminds one of a lonesome mountain-valley. The architecture of the scene is a luminous cloud-picture and the Bacchants swarming on the mountains behold this picture from the heights, — the splendid encirclement in the midst of which is visible the image of Dionysus.

Brought in contact with our learned notions of the elementary artistic processes, this artistic proto-phenomenon, here introduced as an explanation of the tragic chorus, is almost shocking: yet nothing can be more

[4] Zuschauer.
[5] Schauer.

certain than that the poet is a poet only in so far as he sees himself surrounded by forms which live and act before him, and into whose innermost being he penetrates. By reason of a peculiar defect in our modern critical faculty, we are inclined to consider the esthetic proto-phenomenon too complexly, too abstractly. For the true poet a metaphor is not a figure of speech, but a vicarious image which actually hovers before him in place of a concept. To him a character is not an aggregate composed of a number of particular traits, but an organic person pressing himself upon his attention, and differing from the similar vision of the painter only in the continuousness of its life and action. Why does Homer describe much more vividly[6] than all the other poets? Because he contemplates[7] much more. We talk so abstractly about poetry, because we are all bad poets. At bottom the esthetic phenomenon is simple: if a man merely has the faculty of seeing perpetual vitality around him, of living continually surrounded by hosts of spirits, he will be a poet. If he but feels the impulse to transform himself and to speak from out the bodies and souls of others, he will be a dramatist.

The Dionysian excitement is able to inspire a whole mass of men with this artistic faculty of seeing themselves surrounded by such a host of spirits with whom they know themselves to be essentially one. This process of the tragic chorus is the *dramatic* proto-phenomenon: to see yourself transformed before your own eyes, and then to act as if you had actually taken possession of another body and another character. This process stands at the beginning of the development of the drama. Here we have something different from the rhapsodist, who does not unite with his images, but, like the painter, merely views them contemplatively, with detachment. Here we actually have the individual surrendering himself by the fact of his entrance into an alien nature. Moreover, this phenomenon is epidemic in its manifestation: a whole throng experiences this metamorphosis. Hence it is that the dithyramb is essentially different from every other variety of choric song. The virgins, who, laurel branches in hand, solemnly make their way to the temple of Apollo singing a processional hymn, remain what they are and retain their civic names: but the dithyrambic chorus is a chorus of transformed beings, whose civic past and social position are totally forgotten. They have become the timeless servants of their god, living apart from all the life of the community. Every other kind of choric lyric of the Hellenes is nothing but an enormous intensification of the Apollonian unit-singer: while in the dithyramb we have a community of

---

[6] Anschaulicher.
[7] Anschaut.

unconscious actors, who mutually regard themselves as transformed among one another.

This enchantment is the prerequisite for all dramatic art. Under its spell the Dionysian reveler sees himself as a satyr, *and as satyr he in turn beholds the god*, that is, in his transformation he sees a new vision outside him as the Apollonian consummation of his own state. With this new vision the drama completes itself.

According to this view, we must understand Greek tragedy as the Dionysian chorus, disburdening itself again and again in an Apollonian image-world. The choric parts, therefore, with which tragedy is interlaced, are in a sense the maternal womb of the entire so-called dialogue, that is, of the whole stage-world, of the drama proper. In several successive outbursts this primal basis of tragedy releases this vision of the drama, which is a dream-phenomenon throughout, and, as such, epic in character: on the other hand, however, as the objectification of a Dionysian state, it represents not the Apollonian redemption in appearance, but, conversely, the dissolution of the individual and his unification with primordial existence. And so the drama becomes the Apollonian embodiment of Dionysian perceptions and influences, and therefore separates itself by a tremendous gap from the epic.

The *chorus* of the Greek tragedy, the symbol of the collectively excited Dionysian throng, thus finds its full explanation in our conception. Accustomed as we were to the function performed by our modern stage chorus, especially an operatic one, we could never comprehend why the tragic chorus of the Greeks should be older, more primitive, indeed, more important than the "action" proper — as has been so plainly declared by the voice of tradition; whereas, furthermore, we could not reconcile with this traditional primacy and primitiveness the fact that the chorus was composed only of humble, attendant beings — indeed, in the beginning, only of goatlike satyrs; and, finally, there remained the riddle of the orchestra before the scene. We have at last realized that the scene, together with the action, was fundamentally and originally thought of only as a *vision*, that the only reality is just the chorus, which of itself generates the vision and celebrates it with the entire symbolism of dancing, music, and speech. In the vision, this chorus beholds its lord and master Dionysus, and so it is forever a chorus that *serves*; it sees how he, the god, suffers and glorifies himself, and therefore does not itself *act*. But though its attitude towards the god is throughout the attitude of ministration, this is nevertheless the highest, that is, the Dionysian, expression of *Nature*, and therefore, like Nature herself in a state of transport, the chorus utters oracles and wise sayings: as *fellow-sufferer* it is at the same time the *sage* who proclaims truth from out the heart of Nature. Thus, then, originates the fantastic figure, seemingly so discordant, of the wise and inspired satyr, who is at the same time "the dumb man" in contrast to the god: who is the image of Nature and her strongest impulses, the very symbol of Nature, and at the same time the *proclaimer* of her art and vision: musician, poet, dancer, and visionary united in one person.

In accordance with this view, and with tradition, *Dionysus*, the proper stage-hero and focus of vision, is in the remotest period of tragedy not at first actually present, but is only so imagined, which means that tragedy is originally only "chorus" and not "drama." Later on the attempt is made to present the god as real and to display the visionary figure together with its aura of splendor before the eyes of all; here the "drama," in the narrow sense of the term, begins. The dithyrambic chorus is now assigned the task of exciting the minds of the audience to such a pitch of Dionysian frenzy, that, when the tragic hero appears on the stage, they do not see in him an unshapely man wearing a mask, but they see a visionary figure, born as it were of their own ecstasy. Picture Admetus, sunk in profound meditation about his lately departed wife, Alcestis, and quite consuming himself in fancied contemplation. Suddenly the veiled figure of a woman, resembling her in form and gait, is led towards him. Picture his sudden trembling anxiety, his excited comparisons, his instinctive conviction — and we shall have a sensation comparable to that with which the dionysiacally excited spectator saw approaching on the stage, the god with whose sufferings he has already become identified. Involuntarily, he transferred the whole image of the god, fluttering magically before his soul, to this masked figure and resolved its reality as it were into a phantasmal unreality. This is the Apollonian dream-state, in which the world of day is veiled, and a new world, clearer, more intelligible, more vivid and yet more shadowy than the old, is, by a perpetual transformation, born and reborn before our eyes. Accordingly we recognize in tragedy a complete stylistic opposition: the language, color, flexibility and movement of the dialogue fall apart into two entirely separate realms of expression, into the Dionysian lyrics of the chorus on the one hand, and the Apollonian dream-world of the scene on the other. The Apollonian appearances, in which Dionysus objectifies himself, are no longer "ein ewiges Meer, ein wechselnd Weben, ein glühend Leben,"[8] as is the music of the chorus. They are no longer those forces merely felt, but not condensed into a picture, by which the inspired votary of Dionysus divines the proximity of his god. Now the

---

[8] An eternal sea, A weaving, flowing, Life, all glowing. *Faust*, Bayard Taylor's trans.

clearness and firmness of epic form speak to him from the scene; now Dionysus no longer speaks through forces, but as an epic hero, almost with the tongue of Homer.

9

WHATEVER rises to the surface in the dialogue of the Apollonian part of Greek tragedy, appears simple, transparent, beautiful. In this sense the dialogue is a reflection of the Hellene, whose nature reveals itself in the dance, because in the dance while the greatest energy is merely potential, it nevertheless betrays itself in the flexibility and exuberance of movement. The language of the Sophoclean heroes, for instance, surprises us so much by its Apollonian precision and clarity, that we at once think we see into the innermost recesses of their being, not a little astounded that the way thereto is so short. But let us, for the moment, disregard the character of the hero which rises to the surface and grows visible — and which at bottom is nothing but the light-picture cast on a dark wall, that is, appearance through and through. Instead, let us enter into the myth which is projected in these bright mirrorings. We shall suddenly experience a phenomenon which has an inverse relation to one familiar in optics. When, after trying hard to look straight at the sun, we turn away blinded, we have dark-colored spots before our eyes as restoratives, so to speak; while, reversing the colors, those light-picture phenomena of the Sophoclean hero, — in short, the Apollonian of the mask, — are the inevitable consequences of a glance into the secret and terrible things of nature. They are shining spots intended to heal the eye which dire night has seared. Only in this sense can we hope to grasp the true meaning of the serious and significant idea of "Greek cheerfulness"; while no matter where we turn at the present time we encounter the false notion that this cheerfulness results from a state of unendangered comfort.

The most sorrowful figure of the Greek stage, the unfortunate Œdipus, is conceived by Sophocles as the type of the noble man who despite his wisdom is fated to error and misery, but who nevertheless, through his extraordinary sufferings, ultimately exerts a magical, healing effect on all around him, which continues even after his death. The noble man does not sin; this is what the profound poet would tell us. All laws, all natural order, yea, the moral world itself, may be destroyed through his action, but through this very action there is brought into play a higher magic circle of influences which build up a new world on the ruins of the old. This is what the poet, in so far as he is at the same time a religious thinker, wishes to tell us: as poet, he first of all discloses to us a wonderfully complicated legal mystery, which slowly, link by link, the judge to his own destruction unravels. The truly Hellenic delight in this dialectical resolution is so great that a touch of surpassing cheerfulness is thereby communicated to the whole play. This touch everywhere softens the edge of the horrible presuppositions of the plot. In the *Œdipus at Colonus* we find this same cheerfulness, only infinitely transfigured. In contrast to the aged king, burdened with an excess of misery, whose relation to all that befalls him is solely that of a sufferer, we have here a supramundane cheerfulness, descending from a divine sphere and making us feel that in his purely passive attitude the hero achieves his highest activity, whose influence extends far beyond his life, while his earlier conscious thought and striving led him only to passivity. Thus, the legal knot of the Œdipus fable, which to mortal eyes appears impossibly complicated, is slowly unraveled — and at this divine counterpart of dialectic we are filled with a profound human joy. If this explanation does justice to the poet, it may still be asked whether the content of the myth is thereby exhausted; and here it becomes evident that the entire conception of the poet is nothing but the light-picture which, after our glance into the abyss, healing nature holds up to our eyes. Œdipus, murderer of his father, husband of his mother, solver of the riddle of the Sphinx! What is the significance of the mysterious triad of these deeds of destiny? There is, especially in Persia, a primitive popular belief that a wise Magian can be born only of incest. With the riddle-solving and mother-marrying Œdipus in mind, we must immediately interpret this to the effect that wherever by some prophetic and magical power the boundary of the present and future, the inflexible law of individuation and, in general, the intrinsic spell of nature, are broken, an extraordinary counter-naturalness — in this case, incest — must have preceded as a cause; for how else could one force nature to surrender her secrets but by victoriously opposing her by means of the Unnatural? This is the secret which I see involved in the awful triad of the destiny of Œdipus; the very man who solves the riddle of nature — that doubly-constituted Sphinx — must also, as the murderer of his father and husband of his mother, break the holiest laws of nature. Indeed, it seems as if the myth were trying to whisper into our ears the fact that wisdom, especially Dionysian wisdom, is an unnatural abomination; that whoever, through his own knowledge, plunges nature into an abyss of annihilation, must also expect to experience the dissolution of nature in himself. "The sharpness of wisdom turns upon the sage: wisdom is a crime against nature": such are the terrible expressions the myth cries out to us. But the Hellenic poet, like a sunbeam, touches the sublime and terrible Memnonian statue of the myth, and suddenly it begins to sound — in Sophoclean melodies.

Let me now contrast the glory of passivity with the glory of activity which illuminates the *Prometheus* of Æschylus. What Æschylus the thinker had to tell us here, but which as a poet he only allows us to surmise through his symbolic picture, the youthful Goethe has known how to reveal to us in the bold words of his Prometheus: —

> "Hier sitz' ich, forme Menschen
> Nach meinem Bilde,
> Ein Geschlecht, das mir gleich sei,
> Zu leiden, zu weinen,
> Zu geniessen und zu freuen sich,
> Und dein nicht zu achten,
> Wie ich!"[9]

Man, rising to the level of the Titans, acquires his culture by himself, and compels the gods to ally themselves with him, because in his self-sufficient wisdom he holds in his hands their existence and their limitations. The most wonderful thing, however, in this Prometheus fable, which according to its fundamental conception is an essential hymn of impiety, is the profound Æschylean yearning for *justice*. The infinite tragedy of the bold "individual" on the one hand, and the divine necessity and premonition of a twilight of the gods on the other, the force in these two worlds of suffering operating to produce reconciliation, metaphysical oneness — all this strongly suggests the central and main position of the Æschylean view of the world, which sees Moira as eternal justice enthroned over gods and men. Lest we be surprised at the astounding boldness with which Æschylus weighs the Olympian world in his scales of justice, we must always keep in mind that the thinking Greek had an immovably firm substratum of metaphysical thought in his mysteries, and that all his fits or skepticism could be vented upon the Olympians. When he thought of these deities, the Greek artist in particular had an obscure feeling of *mutual* dependency: and it is precisely in the Prometheus of Æschylus that this feeling is symbolized. The Titanic artist discovered in himself a bold confidence in his ability to create men and at least destroy the gods. He might do this by his superior wisdom,

---

[9] "Here I sit, forming mankind In my own image, A race resembling me — To sorrow, to weep, To taste, to have pleasure, And to have no need of thee, Even as I!"

for which, to be sure, he had to atone by eternal suffering. The splendid "I can" of the great genius, bought cheaply even at the price of eternal suffering, the stern pride of the artist: this is the essence and soul of Æschylean poetry, while Sophocles in his Œdipus strikes up as prelude the triumphal chant of the *saint*. But even this interpretation which Æschylus has given to the myth does not reveal the astounding depth of its terror. As a matter of fact, the artist's delight in unfolding, the gayety of artistic creation bidding defiance to all calamity, is actually a shining stellar and nebular image reflected in a black sea of sadness. The story of Prometheus is an original possession of the entire Aryan race, and is documentary evidence of its capacity for the profoundly tragic. Indeed, it is not entirely improbable that this myth has the same characteristic significance for the Aryan genius that the myth of the fall of man has for the Semitic, and that the two are related like brother and sister. The presupposition of the Promethean myth is the transcendent value which a naïve humanity attaches to *fire* as the true palladium of every rising culture. That man, however, should not receive this fire only as a gift from heaven, in the form of the igniting lightning or the warming sunshine, but should, on the contrary, be able to control it at will—this appeared to the reflective primitive man as sacrilege, as robbery of the divine nature. And thus the first philosophical problem at once causes a painful, irreconcilable antagonism between man and God, and puts as it were a mass of rock at the gate of every culture. The best and highest that men can acquire they must obtain by a crime, and then they must in turn endure its consequences, namely, the whole flood of sufferings and sorrows with which the offended divinities *must* requite the nobly aspiring race of man. It is a bitter thought, which, by the *dignity* it confers on crime, contrasts strangely with the Semitic myth of the fall of man, in which curiosity, deception, weakness in the face of temptation, wantonness,—in short, a whole series of preëminently feminine passions,—were regarded as the origin of evil. What distinguishes the Aryan conception is the sublime view of *active sin* as the essential Promethean virtue, and the discovery of the ethical basis of pessimistic tragedy in the *justification* of human evil—of human guilt as well as of the suffering incurred thereby. The pain implicit in the very structure of things—which the contemplative Aryan is not disposed to explain away—the antagonism in the heart of the world, manifests itself to him as a medley of different worlds, for instance, a Divine and a human world, both of which are in the right individually, but which, because they exist separately side by side, must suffer for that very individuation. In the heroic effort towards universality made by the individual, in his attempt to penetrate beyond the bounds of individuation and become himself the *one* world-being, he experiences in himself the primordial contradiction concealed in the essence of things, that is, he trespasses and he suffers. Accordingly crime[10] is understood by the Aryans to be masculine, sin[11] by the Semites to be feminine; just as the original crime is committed by man, the original sin by woman. Besides, as the witches' chorus says:

> "Wir nehmen das nicht so genau:
> Mit tausend Schritten macht's die Frau;
> Doch wie sie auch sich eilen kann
> Mit einem Sprunge macht's der Mann."[12]

He who understands this innermost core of the Prometheus myth — namely, the necessity for crime imposed on the titanically striving individual — will at once feel the un-Apollonian element in this pessimistic representation. For Apollo seeks to calm individual beings precisely by drawing boundary lines between them, and by again and again, with his requirements of self-knowledge and self-control, recalling these bounds to us as the holiest laws of the universe. However, in order that this Apollonian tendency might not congeal the form to Egyptian rigidity and coldness, in order that the effort to prescribe to the individual wave its path and compass might not ruin the motion of the entire lake, the high tide of the Dionysian tendency destroyed from time to time all those little circles in which the one-sided Apollonian "will" sought to confine the Hellenic world. The suddenly swelling Dionysian tide then takes the separate little wave-mountains of individuals on its back, just as the brother of Prometheus, the Titan Atlas, does with the earth. This Titanic impulse, to become as it were the Atlas of all individuals, and on broad shoulders to bear them higher and higher, farther and farther, is what the Promethean and the Dionysian have in common. In this respect the Æschylean Prometheus is a Dionysian mark, while, in the afore-mentioned profound yearning for justice, Æschylus betrays to the intelligent eye his paternal descent from Apollo, the god of individuation, the god who sets the boundaries of justice. And so the double personality of the Æschylean Prometheus, his conjoint Dionysian and Apollonian nature, might be thus expressed in an abstract

---

[10] *Der* Frevel.

[11] *Die* Sünde.

[12] We do not measure with such care: Woman in thousand steps is there, But howsoe'er she hasten may, Man in one leap has cleared the way. *Faust*, Bayard Taylor's trans.

formula: "Whatever exists is alike just and unjust, and in both cases equally justified."

"Das ist deine Welt! Das heisst eine Welt!"[13]

10

THE tradition is undisputed that Greek tragedy in its earliest form had for its sole theme the sufferings of Dionysus, and that for a long time the only stage-hero was simply Dionysus himself. With equal confidence, however, we can assert that, until Euripides, Dionysus never once ceased to be the tragic hero; that in fact all the celebrated figures of the Greek Stage — Prometheus, Œdipus, etc. — are but masks of this original hero, Dionysus. There is godhead behind all these masks; and that is the one essential cause of the typical "ideality," so often wondered at, of these celebrated characters. I know not who it was maintained that all individuals as such are comic and consequently untragic: whence we might infer that the Greeks in general *could* not endure individuals on the tragic stage. And they really seem to have felt this: as, in general, we may note in the Platonic distinction, so deeply rooted in the Hellenic nature, of the "idea" in contrast to the "eidolon," or image. Using Plato's terms we should have to speak of the tragic figures of the Hellenic stage somewhat as follows: the one truly real Dionysus appears in a variety of forms, in the mask of a fighting hero and entangled, as it were, in the net of the individual will. In the latter case the visible god talks and acts so as to resemble an erring, striving, suffering individual. That, generally speaking, he *appears* with such epic precision and clarity is the work of the dream-reading Apollo, who through this symbolic appearance indicates to the chorus its Dionysian state. In reality, however, and behind this appearance, the hero is the suffering Dionysus of the mysteries, the god experiencing in himself the agonies of individuation, of whom wonderful myths tell that as a boy he was torn to pieces by the Titans and has been worshiped in this state as Zagreus: whereby is intimated that this dismemberment, the properly Dionysian *suffering*, is like a transformation into air, water, earth, and fire, that we are therefore to regard the state of individuation as the origin and prime cause of all suffering, as something objectionable in itself. From the smile of this Dionysus

---

[13] There is thy world, and what a world! — *Faust.*

sprang the Olympian gods, from his tears sprang man. In this existence as a dismembered god, Dionysus possesses the dual nature of a cruel barbarized demon and a mild, gentle-hearted ruler. But the hope of the epopts looked towards a new birth of Dionysus, which we must now in anticipation conceive as the end of individuation. It was for this coming third Dionysus that the epopts' stormy hymns of joy resounded. And it is this hope alone that casts a gleam of joy upon the features of a world torn asunder and shattered into individuals: as is symbolized in the myth of Demeter, sunk in eternal sorrow, who *rejoices* again only when told that she may *once more* give birth to Dionysus. This view of things already provides us with all the elements of a profound and pessimistic contemplation of the world, together with the *mystery doctrine of tragedy*: the fundamental knowledge of the oneness of everything existent, the conception of individuation as the prime cause of evil, and of art as the joyous hope that the bonds of individuation may be broken in augury of a restored oneness.

We have already pointed out that the Homeric epos is the poem of Olympian culture, in which this culture has sung its own song of victory over the terrors of the war of the Titans. Under the predominating influence of tragic poetry, these Homeric myths are now born anew; and this metempsychosis reveals that in the meantime the Olympian culture also has been conquered by a still deeper view of things. The insolent Titan Prometheus has announced to his Olympian tormentor that some day the greatest danger will menace his rule, unless Zeus ally with him in time. In Æschylus we perceive the terrified Zeus, fearful of his end, allying himself with the Titan. Thus, the former age of the Titans is once more recovered from Tartarus and brought to the light of day. The philosophy of wild and naked nature beholds with the frank, undissembling gaze of truth the myths of the Homeric world as they dance past: they turn pale, they tremble under the piercing glance of this goddess — till the powerful fist of the Dionysian artist forces them into the service of the new deity. Dionysian truth takes over the entire domain of myth as the symbolism of *its* knowledge. This it makes known partly in the public cult of tragedy and partly in the secret celebration of the dramatic mysteries, but always in the old mythical garb. What power was it that freed Prometheus from his vultures and transformed the myth into a vehicle of Dionysian wisdom? It is the Heracleian power of music: which, having reached its highest manifestation in tragedy, can invest myths with a new and most profound significance. This we have already characterized as the most powerful function of music. For it is the fate of every myth to creep by degrees into the narrow limits of some alleged historical reality, and to be treated by some later generation as a unique fact with historical claims: and the Greeks were already fairly on the way to restamp the whole of their mythical juvenile dream sagaciously and arbitrarily into a historico-pragmatical *juvenile history*. For this is the way in which religions are wont to die out: when under the stern, intelligent eyes of an orthodox dogmatism, the mythical premises of a religion are systematized as a sum total of historical events; when one begins apprehensively to defend the credibility of the myths, while at the same time one opposes any continuation of their natural vitality and growth; when, accordingly, the feeling for myth perishes, and its place is taken by the claim of religion to historical foundations. This dying myth was now seized by the new-born genius of Dionysian music; and in these hands it flourished yet again, with colors such as it had never yet displayed, with a fragrance that awakened a longing anticipation of a metaphysical world. After this final effulgence it collapses, its leaves wither, and soon the mocking Lucians of antiquity catch at the discolored and faded flowers carried away by the four winds. Through tragedy the myth attains its most vital content, its most expressive form; it rises once more like a wounded hero, and its whole excess of strength, together with the philosophic calm of the dying, burns in its eyes with a last powerful gleam.

What didst thou mean, O impious Euripides, in seeking once more to subdue this dying one to your service? Under thy ruthless hands it died: and then thou madest use of counterfeit, masked myth, which like the ape of Heracles could but trick itself out in the old finery. And as myth died in thy hands, so too died the genius of music; though thou didst greedily plunder all the gardens of music — thou didst attain but a counterfeit, masked music. And as thou hast forsaken Dionysus, Apollo hath also forsaken thee; rouse up all the passions from their haunts and conjure them into thy circle, sharpen and whet thy sophistical dialectic for the speeches of thy heroes — thy very heroes have but counterfeit, masked passions, and utter but counterfeit, masked words.

11

GREEK tragedy met an end different from that of her older sister arts: she died by suicide, in consequence of an irreconcilable conflict. Accordingly she died tragically, while all the others passed away calmly and beautifully at a ripe old age. If it be consonant with a happy natural state to take leave of life easily, leaving behind a fair posterity, the closing period of these older arts exhibits such a happy natural state: slowly they sink from sight, and before their dying eyes already stand their fairer progeny, who impatiently, with a bold gesture, lift up their heads. But when Greek tragedy died, there rose everywhere the deep feeling of an immense void. Just as the Greek sailors in the time of Tiberius once heard upon a lonesome island the thrilling cry, "Great Pan is dead": so now through the Hellenic world there sounded the grievous lament: "Tragedy is dead! Poetry itself has perished with her! Away with you, ye pale, stunted epigones! Away to Hades, that ye may for once eat your fill of the crumbs of your former masters!"

And when after this death a new Art blossomed forth which revered tragedy as her ancestress and mistress, it was observed with horror that she did indeed bear the features of her mother, but that they were the very features the latter had exhibited in her long death-struggle. It was Euripides who fought this death-struggle of tragedy; the later art is known as the *New Attic Comedy*. In it the degenerate form of tragedy lived on as a monument of its painful and violent death.

This connection helps to explain the passionate attachment that the poets of the New Comedy felt for Euripides; so that we are no longer surprised at the wish of Philemon, who would have let himself be hanged at once, merely that he might visit Euripides in the lower world: if he could only be certain that the deceased still had possession of his reason. But if we desire, as briefly as possible, and without claiming to say anything exhaustive, to characterize what Euripides has in common with Menander and Philemon, and what appealed to them so strongly as worthy of imitation, it is sufficient to say that Euripides brought the *spectator* upon the stage. He who has perceived the material out of which the Promethean tragic writers prior to Euripides formed their heroes, and how remote from their purpose it was to bring the true mask of reality on the stage, will also be able to explain the utterly opposite tendency of Euripides. Through him the average man forced his way from the spectators' benches on to the stage itself; the mirror in which formerly only grand and bold traits were represented now showed the painful fidelity that conscientiously reproduces even the abortive outlines of nature. Odysseus, the typical Hellene of the older art, now sank, in the hands of the new poets, to the figure of the Græculus, who, as the good-naturedly cunning house-slave, henceforth occupies the center of dramatic interest. What Euripides claims credit for in Aristophanes' *Frogs*, namely, that his household medicines have freed tragic art from its pompous corpulency, is apparent above all in his tragic heroes. The spectator now actually saw and heard his double on the Euripidean stage, and rejoiced that he could talk so well. But this joy was not all: you could even learn of Euripides how to speak. He prides himself upon this in his contest with Æschylus: from him the people have learned how to observe, debate, and draw conclusions according to the rules of art and with the cleverest sophistries. In general, through this revolution of the popular speech, he had made the New Comedy possible. For henceforth it was no longer a secret, how — and with what wise maxims — the commonplace was to express itself on the stage. Civic mediocrity, on which Euripides built all his political hopes, was now given a voice, while heretofore the demigod in tragedy and the drunken satyr, or demiman, in comedy, had determined the character of the language. And so the Aristophanean Euripides prides himself on having portrayed the common, familiar, everyday life and activities of the people, about which all are qualified to pass judgment. If now the entire populace philosophizes, manages land and goods and conducts law-suits with unheard-of circumspection, the glory is all his, together with the splendid results of the wisdom with which he has inoculated the rabble.

It was to a populace thus prepared and illuminated that that New Comedy could now address itself, of which Euripides had become as it were the chorus-master; only that this time the chorus of spectators had to be trained. As soon as this chorus was trained to sing in the Euripidean key, there arose that drama which resembles a game of chess — the New Comedy, with its perpetual triumphs of cunning and artfulness. But Euripides — the chorus-master — was still praised continually: indeed, people would have killed themselves in order to learn still more from him, if they had not known that tragic poets were quite as dead as tragedy. But with that death the Hellene had given up his belief in immortality; not only his belief in an ideal past, but also his belief in an ideal future. The words of the well-known epitaph, "frivolous and capricious as an old man," also suit senile Hellenism. The passing moment, wit, levity, and caprice are its highest deities; the fifth estate, that of the slaves, now comes into power, at least in sentiment: and if we may still speak at all of "Greek cheerfulness," it is the cheerfulness of the slave who has nothing of consequence to be responsible for, nothing great to strive for, and who cannot value anything in the past or future higher than the present. It was this semblance of "Greek cheerfulness" which so aroused the deep-minded and formidable natures of the first four centuries of the Christian era: this womanish flight from seriousness and terror, this craven satisfaction with easy enjoyment, seemed to them not only contemptible, but a specifically anti-Christian sentiment. And to influence of that sentiment we must ascribe the fact that the conception of Greek antiquity, which endured for centuries, preserved with almost unconquerable persistency that feverish hue of cheerfulness — as if there had never been a Sixth Century with its birth of tragedy, its Mysteries, its Pythagoras and Heraclitus, as if the very art-works of that great period did not at all exist, though these phenomena can hardly be explained as having originated in any such senile and slavish love of existence and cheerfulness, and though they indicate as the source of their being an altogether different conception of the world.

The assertion made above, that Euripides brought the spectator on the stage that he might better qualify him to pass judgment on the drama, makes it appear as if the old or tragic art had always been in a false relation to the spectator; and one might be tempted to extol as an advance over Sophocles the radical tendency of Euripides to produce a proper relation between art-work and public. But "public," after all, is only a word. In no sense is it a homogeneous and constant quantity. Why should the artist be bound to accommodate himself to a power whose strength lies merely in numbers? And if, by virtue of his endow-ments and aspirations, he should feel himself superior to every one of these spectators, how should he feel greater respect for the collective expression of all these subordinate capacities than for the relatively highest-endowed individual spectator? In truth, if ever a Greek artist throughout a long life treated his public with arrogance and self-sufficiency, it was Euripides. When the rabble threw themselves at his feet, he openly and with sublime defiance attacked his own tendency, the very tendency with which he had won over the masses. If this genius had had the slightest respect for the noise the mob makes, he would have broken down long before the middle of his career beneath the heavy blows of his own failures. These considerations make it clear that our formula — namely, that Euripides brought the spectator on the stage in order to make him truly competent to pass judgment — was but a provisional one, and that therefore we must penetrate more deeply to understand his tendency. Conversely, it is known beyond any question that Æschylus and Sophocles during the whole of their lives, and indeed, long after their deaths, were in complete possession of the people's favor, and that therefore in the case of these fore-runners of Euripides there was never any question of a false relation between art-work and public. What was it then that thus forcibly drove this artist, so richly endowed, so constantly impelled to production, from the path warmed by the sun of the greatest names in poetry and covered by the cloudless heaven of popular favor? What strange consideration for the spectator led him to oppose the spectator? How could he, out of too great a respect for his public — despise his public?

Euripides — and this is the solution of the riddle just propounded — undoubtedly felt himself, as a poet, superior to the masses in general;

but to two of his spectators he did not feel superior. He brought the masses upon the stage; and these two spectators he revered as the only competent judges and masters of his art. Complying with their directions and admonitions, he transferred the entire world of sentiments, passions, and experiences, hitherto present at every festival representation as the invisible chorus on the spectators' benches, into the souls of his stage-heroes. He yielded to their demands, too, when for these new characters he sought out a new language and a new accent. Only in their voices could he hear any conclusive verdict on his work, and also the cheering promise of triumph when he found himself as usual condemned by the public judgment.

Of these two spectators, one is — Euripides himself, Euripides *as thinker*, not as poet. It might be said of him, as of Lessing, that his copious fund of *critical* talent, if it did not create, at least constantly stimulated a corresponding and productive *artistic* impulse. With this faculty, with all the clarity and dexterity of his critical temper, Euripides had sat in the theater and striven to recognize in the masterpieces of his great predecessors, as in faded paintings, feature after feature, line after line. And here he had experienced something which any one initiated in the deeper secrets of Æschylean tragedy might have foretold. He observed something incommensurable in every feature and in every line of the tragedy, a certain deceptive distinctness and at the same time a mysterious depth, almost an infinitude, of background. Even the clearest figure always had a comet's tail attached to it, which seemed to suggest the uncertain, the nebulous. A similar twilight shrouded the structure of the drama, especially the element of the function of the chorus. And how dubious remained the solution of the ethical problems! How questionable the treatment of the myths! How unequal the distribution of good and bad fortune! In the very language of the Old Tragedy there was much that was objectionable to him, or at least puzzling; especially he encountered too much pomp for simple affairs, too many tropes and monstrous expressions to suit the plainness of the characters. So he sat in the theater, pondering uneasily, and as a spectator he confessed to himself that he did not understand his great predecessors. If, however, it was his opinion that the understanding was the essential root of all enjoyment and creation, he must inquire, he must look about to see whether any one else had the same opinion, and whether they also felt this incommensurability. But most people, and among them the finest individuals, answered him only with a distrustful smile; while none could explain why the great masters were still in the right despite his scruples and objections. And in this state of torment, he found *that other spectator*, who did not comprehend tragedy, and therefore did not esteem it. Allied with him, in solitary state, he could now venture to begin the terrific struggle against the art of Æschylus and Sophocles — not as a polemist, but as a dramatic poet, who would oppose *his own* conception of tragedy to the traditional one.

12

BEFORE we name this other spectator, let us pause here a moment in order to recall to our minds our own previously described impression of the discordant and incommensurable elements in the genius of Æschylean tragedy. Let us think of our own surprise at the *chorus* and the *tragic hero* of that tragedy, neither of which we could reconcile with our own customs any more than with tradition — till we rediscovered this duality itself as the origin and essence of Greek tragedy, as the expression of two interwoven artistic impulses, *the Apollonian and the Dionysian.*

To separate this primitive and all-powerful Dionysian element from tragedy, and to construct a new and purified form on the basis of an un-Dionysian art, morality, and conception of the world — this is the tendency of Euripides as it is now clearly revealed to us.

In the evening of his life, Euripides himself composed a myth in which he urgently propounded to his contemporaries the question as to the value and significance of this tendency. Is the Dionysian entitled to exist at all? Should it not be forcibly uprooted from Hellenic soil? Certainly, the poet tells us, if it were only possible: but the god Dionysus is too powerful; his most intelligent adversary — like Pentheus in the *Bacchæ* — is unwittingly enchanted by him, and in this enchantment runs to meet his fate. The judgment of the two old prophets, Cadmus and Tiresias, seems also to be the judgment of the aged poet: that the reflection of the wisest individuals does not overthrow old popular traditions, nor the perpetually self-propagating worship of Dionysus; that in fact it is to our interest to display at the very least a diplomatically cautious concern in the presence of such strange forces: although there is always the possibility that the god may take offense at such lukewarm participation, and eventually transform the diplomat — in this case Cadmus — into a dragon. This is what we are told by a poet who opposed Dionysus with heroic valor throughout a long life — and who finally ended his career with a glorification of his adversary, and with suicide, like one staggering from giddiness, who, to escape the horrible vertigo he can no longer endure, casts himself from a tower. This tragedy — the *Bacchæ* — is a protest against the practicability of his own tendency; but alas, it has already been put into practice! The surprising thing had happened: when the poet recanted, his tendency had already conquered. Dionysus had already been scared from the tragic stage; he had been scared by a demonic power speaking through Euripides. For even Euripides was, in a sense, only a mask: the deity that spoke through him was neither Dionysus nor Apollo. It was an altogether new-born demon. And it was called *Socrates*. Thus we have a new antithesis — the Dionysian and the Socratic; and on that antithesis the art of Greek tragedy was wrecked. In vain does Euripides seek to comfort us by his recantation. It avails not: the most magnificent temple lies in ruins. Of what use is the lamentation of the destroyer, of what use his confession that it was the most beautiful of all temples? And even if Euripides has been punished by being changed into a dragon by the art-critics of all ages — who could be content with so miserable a compensation?

Let us now examine this *Socratic* tendency with which Euripides combated and vanquished Æschylean tragedy.

We must first ask ourselves, what could be the aim of the Euripidean design, which, in its most ideal form, would wish to base drama exclusively on the un-Dionysian? What other form of drama still remained, if it was not to be born of the womb of music, in the mysterious twilight of the Dionysian? Only *the dramatized epos*: in which Apollonian domain of art the *tragic* effect is of course unattainable. For it is not bound up with the subject-matter of the events represented; indeed, I maintain that it would have been impossible for Goethe in his projected *Nausikaa* to have rendered tragically effective the suicide of the idyllic being, the scene which was to have completed the fifth act. So extraordinary is the power of the epic-Apollonian representation, that before our very eyes it transforms the most terrible things by the joy in appearance and in redemption through appearance. The poet of the dramatized epos cannot blend completely with his pictures any more than the epic rhapsodist can. He is still just the calm, unmoved embodiment of Contemplation whose wide eyes see the picture *before* them. The actor in this dramatized epos still remains fundamentally a rhapsodist: the consecration of the inner dream lies on all his actions, so that he is never wholly an actor.

How, then, is the Euripidean play related to this ideal of the Apollonian drama? Just as the younger rhapsodist is related to the solemn rhapsodist of the old time. In the Platonic *Ion*, the former describes his own nature as follows: "When I am saying anything sad, my eyes fill with tears; when, however, I am saying something awful and terrible, then my hair stands on end with fright and my heart beats quickly." Here we no longer remark anything of the epic absorption in appearance, or of the dispassionate coolness of the true actor, who precisely in his highest activity is wholly appearance and joy in appearance. Euripides is that actor whose heart beats, whose hair stands on end; as Socratic thinker he designs the plan, as passionate actor he executes it. Neither in the designing nor in the execution is he a pure artist. And so the Euripidean drama is a thing both cool and fiery, equally capable of freezing and burning. It is impossible for it to attain the Apollonian effect of the epos, while, on the other hand, it has alienated itself as much as possible from Dionysian elements. Now, in order to develop at all, it requires new stimulants, which can no longer lie within the sphere of the two unique art-impulses, the Apollonian and the Dionysian. These stimulants are cool, paradoxical *thoughts*, replacing Apollonian intuitions — and fiery *passions*, replacing Dionysian ecstasies; and, it may be added, thoughts and passions copied very realistically and in no sense suffused with the atmosphere of art.

Accordingly, having perceived this much, that Euripides did not succeed in establishing the drama exclusively on an Apollonian basis, but rather that his un-Dionysian inclinations deviated into a naturalistic and inartistic tendency, we should now be able to get a nearer view of the character of *esthetic Socratism*, whose supreme law reads about as follows: "To be beautiful everything must be intelligible," as the counterpart to the Socratic identity: "Knowledge is virtue." With this canon in his hands, Euripides measures all the separate elements of the drama — language, characters, dramaturgic structure, and choric music — and corrects them according to his principle. The poetic deficiency and degeneration, which we are so often wont to impute to Euripides in comparison with Sophocles, is for the most part the product of this penetrating critical process, this daring intelligibility. The Euripidean *prologue* may serve as an example of the results of this rationalistic method. Nothing could be more antithetical to the technique of our own stage than the prologue in the drama of Euripides. For a single person to appear at the outset of the play telling us who he is, what precedes the action, what has happened so far, even what will happen in the course of the play, would be condemned by a modern playwright as a willful, inexcusable abandonment of the effect of suspense. We know everything that is going to happen; who cares to wait till it actually does happen? — considering, moreover, that here we do not by any means have the exciting relation of a prophetic dream to a reality taking place later on. But Euripides' speculations took a different turn. The effect of tragedy never depended on epic suspense, on a fascinating uncertainty as to what is to happen now and afterwards: but rather on the great rhetorical-lyric scenes in which the passion and dialectic of the chief hero swelled to a broad and mighty stream. Everything was directed toward pathos, not action: and whatever was not directed toward pathos was considered objectionable. But what interferes most with the hearer's pleasurable satisfaction in such scenes is a missing link, a gap in the texture of the previous history. So long as the spectator has to divine the meaning of this or that person, or the presuppositions of this or that conflict of views and inclinations, his complete absorption in the activities and sufferings of the chief characters is impossible, as is likewise breathless fellow-feeling and fellow-fearing. The Æschylean-Sophoclean tragedy employed the most ingenious devices in the initial scenes to place in the spectator's hands, as if by chance, all the threads necessary for a complete understanding: a trait whereby that noble artistry is approved, which as it were masks the *inevitably* formal element, and makes it appear something accidental. Notwithstanding this, Euripides thought he observed that during these first scenes the spectator was so peculiarly anxious to make out the problem of the previous history, that the poetic beauties and pathos of the exposition were lost to him. Accordingly he put the prologue even before the exposition, and placed it in the mouth of a person who could be trusted: some deity had often as it were to guarantee the particulars of the tragedy to the public, to remove every doubt as to the reality of the myth, just as did Descartes who could prove the reality of the empirical world only by appealing to the truthfulness of God and His inability to utter falsehood. Euripides makes use of this same divine truthfulness once more at the close of his drama, in order to reassure the public as to the future of his heroes; this is the task of the notorious *deus ex machina*. Between this epic retrospect and epic prospect, is placed the dramatico-lyric present, the "drama" as such.

Thus Euripides as a poet is essentially an echo of his own conscious knowledge; and it is precisely on this account that he occupies such a notable position in the history of Greek art. With reference to his critical-productive activity, he must often have felt that he ought to make objective in drama the words at the beginning of the essay of Anaxagoras: "In the beginning all things were mixed together; then came the understanding and created order." Anaxagoras with his "nous" is said to have appeared among philosophers as the only sober person amid a crowd of drunken ones. Euripides may also have conceived his relation to the other tragic poets under a similar figure. As long as the sole ruler and disposer of the universe, the *nous*, remained excluded from artistic activity, things were all mixed together in a primeval chaos. This was what Euripides was obliged to think; and so, as the first "sober" one among them, he was bound to condemn the "drunken" poets. Sophocles said of Æschylus that he did what was right, though he did it unconsciously. This would surely never have been the opinion of Euripides. He would have said, on the contrary, that Æschylus, *because* he created unconsciously, did what was *wrong*. Similarly the divine Plato for the most part speaks but ironically of the creative faculty of the poet, in so far as it is not conscious insight, and places it on a par with the gift of the soothsayer and dream-interpreter. The intimation is that the poet is incapable of composing until he has become unconscious and bereft of reason. Like Plato, Euripides undertook to show to the world the reverse of the "unintelligent" poet; his esthetic principle that "to be beautiful everything must be known" is, as I have said, the parallel to the Socratic, "to be good everything must be known." So that we may consider Euripides as the poet of esthetic Socratism. But Socrates was that *second spectator* who did not comprehend and therefore did not esteem the Old Tragedy; in alliance with him Euripides dared to be the herald of a new art. If it was this then, that destroyed the older tragedy in general, it follows that esthetic Socratism was the fatal principle; but in so far as the struggle is directed against the *Dionysian element* in the older tragedy, we may recognize in Socrates the opponent of Dionysus. He is the new Orpheus rebelling against Dionysus, and although he is destined to be torn to pieces by the Mænads of the Athenian court, yet he puts to flight the overpowerful god himself. The latter, you will recall, fleeing from Lycurgus, the King of Edoni, sought refuge in the depths of the ocean — or, in this case, in the mystical flood of a secret cult which gradually overran the earth.

13

THAT Socrates was closely related to the tendency of Euripides did not escape the notice of contemporaneous antiquity. The most eloquent expression of this felicitous insight was the story current in Athens that Socrates used to help Euripides in poetizing. Whenever an occasion arose to enumerate the popular agitators of the day, the adherents of the "good old times" would mention both names in the same breath. To the influence of Socrates and Euripides they attributed the fact that the old Marathonian stalwart capacity of body and soul was being sacrificed more and more to a dubious enlightenment that involved the progressive degeneration of the physical and mental powers. It is in this tone, half indignant, half contemptuous, that Aristophanic comedy is wont to speak of both of them — to the consternation of modern men, who are quite willing to give up Euripides, but who cannot help being amazed that Socrates should appear in the comedies of Aristophanes as the first and leading *sophist*, as the mirror and epitome of all sophistical tendencies. The result of their bewilderment is that they give themselves the unique consolation of putting Aristophanes himself in the pillory, as a dissolute, lying Alcibiades of poetry. Without here defending the profound insight of Aristophanes against such attacks, I shall now continue to show, by means of the sentiments of the time, the close connection between Socrates and Euripides. With this in view, we must remember particularly that Socrates, as an opponent of tragic art, refrained from patronizing tragedy, but that he appeared among the spectators only when a new play of Euripides was to be performed. Most famous of all, however, is the juxtaposition of the two names by the Delphic oracle, which designated Socrates as the wisest of men, but at the same time decided that the second prize in the contest of wisdom belonged to Euripides.

Sophocles was named third in order of rank; he who could pride himself that, as compared with Æschylus, he did what was right, and moreover did so because he *knew* what the right was. Evidently it is merely the degree of clearness of this *knowledge* which distinguishes these three men in common as the three "knowing ones" of their time.

The most decisive word, however, for this new and unprecedented value set upon knowledge and insight was spoken by Socrates when he found that he was the only one who acknowledged to himself that he *knew nothing*; for in his critical peregrinations through Athens, he called on the greatest statesmen, orators, poets, and artists, and everywhere he discovered the conceit of knowledge. To his astonishment he perceived that all these celebrities were without a proper and sure insight, even with regard to their own professions, and that they practiced them only by instinct. "Only by instinct": with this phrase we touch upon the heart and core of the Socratic tendency. With it Socratism condemns existing art as well as existing ethics. Wherever Socratism turns its searching eyes it sees lack of insight, it sees the force of illusion; and from this lack it infers the essential perversity and objectionableness of existing conditions. From this point onwards, Socrates conceives it as his duty to correct existence; and, with an air of irreverence and superiority, as the precursor of an altogether different culture, art, and morality, he enters single-handed into a world, to touch whose very hem would give us the greatest happiness.

For an extraordinary hesitancy always seizes upon us with regard to Socrates. Again and again we are impelled to ascertain the sense and purpose of the most puzzling phenomenon of antiquity. Who is this that dares single-handed to disown the Greek genius, which, as Homer, Pindar, and Æschylus, as Phidias, as Pericles, as Pythia and Dionysus, as the deepest abyss and the highest height, compels our wondering admiration? What demonic power is this which dares spill this magic draught in the dust? What demigod is this to whom the chorus of spirits of the noblest of mankind must call out: "Weh! Weh! Du hast sie zerstört, die schöne Welt, mit mächtiger Faust: sie stürzt, sie zerfällt!"[14]

We are offered a key to the character of Socrates by the wonderful phenomenon which he calls his dæmon. In exceptional circumstances, when his gigantic intellect begins to fail him, he receives a secure support in the utterances of a divine voice which manifests itself at such moments. This voice, whenever it comes, always *dissuades*. In this utterly abnormal nature instinctive wisdom only appears in order to *hinder* here and there the progress of conscious perception. Whereas in all productive men it is instinct that is the creatively affirmative force, and consciousness that acts critically and dissuasively; with Socrates it is instinct that becomes critic, and consciousness that becomes creator — a perfect monstrosity *per defectum!* And we do indeed observe here a monstrous *defectus* of all mystical aptitude so that Socrates might be called the typical *non-mystic*, in whom, through a superfœtation, the logical nature is developed, to the same excessive degree as instinctive wisdom is developed in the mystic. Unlike his instinct, however, the logic of Socrates was absolutely prevented from turning against itself; in its unimpeded flow it manifests a native power such as we meet with, to our awe and surprise, only among the very greatest instinctive forces. Any one who has experienced even a breath of the divine naïveté and security of the Socratic way of life in the Platonic writings, will also feel that the enormous driving-wheel of logical Socratism is in motion, as it were, *behind* Socrates, and that it must be viewed through Socrates as through a shadow. And that he himself had a premonition of this relationship is apparent from the dignified seriousness with which he everywhere, even before his judges, insists on his divine calling. It is really as impossible to refute him here as to approve of his instinct-disintegrating influence. In view of this indissoluble conflict, when he had at last been brought before the forum of the Greek state, there was only one kind of punishment demanded, namely, exile. He might have been sped across the borders as something thoroughly enigmatical, inexplicable, and impossible to characterize, and so posterity would never have been justified in charging the Athenians with an igno-

---

[14] Woe! Woe! Thou hast it destroyed, The beautiful world; With powerful fist; In ruin 'tis hurled! *Faust*, Bayard Taylor's trans.

minious deed. But that the sentence of death, and not mere exile, was pronounced upon him, seems to have been the work of Socrates himself, who encountered the decree with perfect awareness and without the natural fear of death. He met his death with the calmness with which, according to Plato's description, he, last of the revelers, leaves the Symposium at dawn to begin a new day; while his sleepy fellow-banqueters remain behind on the couches and the floor, to dream of Socrates, the true eroticist. *The dying Socrates* became the new ideal of the noble Greek youths, — an ideal they had never yet beheld, — and above all, the typical Hellenic youth, Plato, prostrated himself before this scene with all the burning devotion of his visionary soul.

14

LET us now imagine the one great Cyclops eye of Socrates fixed on tragedy, an eye in which the fine frenzy of artistic enthusiasm had never glowed. To this eye was denied the pleasure of gazing into the Dionysian abysses. For what was it bound to see in the "sublime and greatly lauded" tragic art, as Plato called it? A thing devoid of sense, full of causes apparently without effects, and effects apparently without causes; the whole, moreover, so motley and diversified that though it could not but be repugnant to a thoughtful mind, it was a dangerous incentive for sensitive and irritable souls. We know what was the only kind of poetry he understood: the *Æsopian fable:* and this he favored no doubt with the good-natured acquiescence with which the good honest Gellert sings the praise of poetry in the fable of the bee and the hen: —

> "Du siehst an mir, wozu es nutzt,
> Dem, der nicht viel Verstand besitzt,
> Die Wahrheit durch ein Bild zu sagen."[15]

But it seemed to Socrates that tragic art did not even "tell the truth": not to mention the fact that it addressed itself to him who has "no great understanding." Consequently, it did not recommend itself to the philosopher: a twofold reason for shunning it. Like Plato, he reckoned it among the seductive arts which portray only the agreeable, not the useful; and hence he required of his disciples abstinence and strict separation from such unphilosophical temptations, with such success

---

[15] Through me, you may observe how useful it is to tell the truth to those of no great understanding, by means of a parable.

that the youthful tragic poet Plato first of all burned his poems that he might become a student of Socrates. But where unconquerable natural tendencies struggled against the Socratic maxims, their power, together with the momentum of his mighty character, was still enough to force poetry itself into new and hitherto unknown channels.

An instance of this is the aforesaid Plato, Plato who in condemning tragedy and art in general certainly did not lag behind the naïve cynicism of his master, was nevertheless by sheer artistic necessity constrained to create an art-form which is essentially related to those very forms of art which he repudiated. Plato's main objection to the old art — that it is the imitation of a phantom,[16] and hence belongs to a sphere still lower than the empiric world — could not at all be directed against the new art: and so we find Plato endeavoring to go beyond reality and to represent the idea which underlies this pseudo-reality. But Plato, the thinker, thereby arrived by a roundabout road at the very point where he had always been at home as poet, and from which Sophocles and all the older artists had solemnly protested against that objection. If tragedy had absorbed into itself all the earlier varieties of art, the same might also be said in an unusual sense of the Platonic dialogue, which, a mixture of all the then existent forms and styles, hovers midway between narrative, lyric and drama, between prose and poetry, and so has also broken loose from the older strict law of unity of linguistic form. This tendency was carried still farther by the *Cynic* writers, who in the greatest stylistic medley, oscillating between prose and metrical forms, realized also the literary picture of the "raving Socrates" whom they were wont to represent in real life. The Platonic dialogue was a sort of boat in which the shipwrecked ancient poetry was rescued with all her children: crowded into a narrow space and timidly submissive to the single pilot, Socrates, they now launched forth into a new world, which never tired of looking at the fantastic spectacle of this procession. The fact is that Plato has given to all posterity the prototype of a new art-form, the prototype of the *novel*: which may be described as an infinitely developed Æsop fable, in which poetry holds the same rank with reference to dialectic philosophy as this same philosophy held for many centuries with reference to theology: that is to say, the rank of *ancilla*. This was the new position into which Plato, under the pressure of the dæmon-inspired Socrates, forced poetry.

Here *philosophic thought* overgrows art and compels it to cling close to the trunk of dialectic. The *Apollonian* tendency has withdrawn into the shell of logical schematism; just as we noticed something analogous

---

[16] Scheinbild.

in the case of Euripides (and moreover a transformation of the *Dionysian* into the naturalistic emotion). Socrates, the dialectical hero of the Platonic drama, reminds us of the kindred nature of the Euripidean hero, who must defend his actions with arguments and counter-arguments, and who thereby so often incurs the danger of forfeiting our tragic pity; for who could mistake the *optimistic* element in the essence of dialectics, which celebrates a triumph with every conclusion, and can breathe only in cool clearness and consciousness: the optimistic element, which, having once forced its way into tragedy must gradually pass its Dionysian bounds, and necessarily impel it to self-destruction — even to the death-leap into the bourgeois drama. Let us but realize the consequences of the Socratic maxims: "Virtue is knowledge; man sins only from ignorance; he who is virtuous is happy." In these three fundamental forms of optimism lies the death of tragedy. For the virtuous hero must now be a dialectician; there must now be a necessary, visible connection between virtue and knowledge, between belief and morality. The transcendental justice of Æschylus is now degraded to the superficial and audacious principle of "poetic justice" with its customary *deus ex machina*.

In the light of this new Socratic-optimistic stage-world, what becomes of the *chorus* and, in general, of the entire Dionyso-musical substratum of tragedy? The chorus is something accidental, a readily dispensed-with vestige of the origin of tragedy; while, as a matter of fact, we have seen that the chorus can be understood only as the *cause* of tragedy, and of the tragic in general. This perplexity in regard to the chorus already manifests itself in Sophocles — an important indication that even with him the Dionysian basis of tragedy is already beginning to break down. He no longer dares to entrust to the chorus the main share of the effect, but he limits its sphere to such an extent that it now appears almost coördinate with the actors, just as if it were elevated from the orchestra into the scene: whereby of course its character is completely destroyed, notwithstanding that Aristotle countenances this very theory of the chorus. This alteration in the position of the chorus, which Sophocles at any rate recommended by his practice, and, according to tradition, even by a treatise, is the first step towards its destruction, the phases of which follow one another with alarming rapidity in Euripides, Agathon, and the New Comedy. Optimistic dialectic drives *music* out of tragedy with the scourge of its syllogisms: that is, it destroys the essence of tragedy, which can be interpreted only as a manifestation and illustration of Dionysian states, as the visible symbolizing of music, as the dream-world of Dionysian ecstasy.

If, therefore, we must assume an anti-Dionysian tendency operating even before Socrates, which merely received in him a uniquely great expression, we must not draw back before the question as to what such a phenomenon as that of Socrates indicates: whom in view of the Platonic dialogues we are certainly not entitled to regard as a purely disintegrating, negative force. And though there can be no doubt that the most immediate effect of the Socratic impulse tended to the dissolution of Dionysian tragedy, yet a profound experience in Socrates' own life impels us to ask whether there is *necessarily* only an antagonistic relation between Socratism and art, and whether the birth of an "artistic Socrates" is in general a contradiction in terms.

For that despotic logician had now and then with respect to art the feeling of a gap, a void, a feeling of misgiving, of a possibly neglected duty. As he tells his friends in prison, there often came to him one and the same dream-apparition, which kept constantly repeating to him: "Socrates, practice music." Up to his very last days he comforts himself with the statement that his philosophizing is the highest form of art; he finds it hard to believe that a deity should remind him of the "common, popular music." Finally, when in prison and in order that he may thoroughly unburden his conscience, he consents to practice also this music for which he has but little respect. And in this mood he composes a poem on Apollo and turns a few Æsopian fables into verse. It was something akin to the demonic warning voice which urged him to these practices; it was due to his Apollonian insight that, like a barbaric king, he did not understand the noble image of a god and was in danger of sinning against a deity—through his lack of understanding. The voice of the Socratic dream-vision is the only sign of doubt as to the limits of logic. "Perhaps"—thus he must have asked himself—"what is not intelligible to me is not therefore unintelligible? Perhaps there is a realm of wisdom from which the logician is shut out? Perhaps art is even a necessary correlative of, and supplement to, science?"

15

WITH reference to these last weighty questions we must now explain how the influence of Socrates (extending to the present moment, indeed, to all futurity) has spread over posterity like an ever-increasing shadow in the evening sun, and how this influence again and again involves a regeneration of *art* — yea, of art already in the most metaphysical, broadest and profoundest sense — and how its own eternity is also a warrant for the eternity of art.

Before this could be perceived, before the intrinsic dependence of every art on the Greeks, from Homer to Socrates, was conclusively demonstrated, we had to have the same experience with regard to these Greeks as the Athenians had with regard to Socrates. Nearly every age and stage of culture has at some time or other sought with deep irritation to free itself from the Greeks, because in their presence everything self-achieved, sincerely admired and apparently quite original, seemed suddenly to lose life and color, to shrink to an abortive copy, even to caricature. And so time after time hearty resentment breaks forth against this presumptuous little nation, which for all time dared to designate everything not native as "barbaric." Who are they, one asks, who, though they have nothing to show but an ephemeral historical splendor, ridiculously restricted institutions, a dubious excellence in their customs, and the stigma attaching to ugly vices, yet lay claim to the dignity and preëminence among peoples to which genius is entitled among the masses? What a pity we have not been fortunate enough to find the cup of hemlock with which we might very simply rid ourselves of such a character: for all the poison which envy, calumny, and rankling resentment created within themselves have not been able to destroy that self-sufficient grandeur! And so one feels ashamed and afraid in the presence of the Greeks, unless one prizes truth above all things; unless one dares acknowledge to one's self this truth, that the Greeks, as charioteers, hold the reins of our own and every other culture, but that almost always chariot and horses are of too poor material and hardly up to the glory of their guides. Unless we acknowledge this, who will deem it sport to run such a team into an abyss which they themselves could clear with the leap of Achilles?

In order to endow Socrates with the dignity of such a leading position, it is enough to recognize in him a type unheard of before him, the type of the *theoretical man*. Our next task will be to obtain an insight into the meaning and purpose of this theoretical man. Like the artist, the theorist finds an infinite satisfaction in the present, and, like the former also, this satisfaction protects him from the practical ethics of pessimism with its lynx eyes shining only in the dark. Whenever the truth is unveiled, the artist will always cling with rapt gaze to whatever still remains veiled after the unveiling; but the theoretical man gets his enjoyment and satisfaction out of the cast-off veil. He finds his highest pleasure in the process of a continuously successful unveiling effected through his own unaided efforts. There would have been no science if it had been concerned only with that *one* naked goddess and nothing else. For then its disciples would have felt like those who wished to dig a hole straight through the earth: each one of them perceives that with his utmost lifelong efforts he can excavate but a very small portion of the enormous depth, and this is filled up again before his eyes by the labors of his successor, so that a third man seems to be doing a sensible thing in selecting a new spot for his attempts at tunneling. Now suppose some one shows conclusively that the antipodal goal cannot be attained thus directly. Who will then still care to toil on in the old depths, unless in the meantime he has learned to content himself with finding precious stones or discovering natural laws? For this reason Lessing, the most honest of theoretical men, boldly said that he cared more for the search after truth than for truth itself: in saying which, he revealed the fundamental secret of science, to the astonishment, and indeed, to the anger of scientists. Well, to be sure, beside this detached perception there stands, with an air of great frankness, if not presumption, a profound *illusion* which first came to birth in the person of Socrates. This illusion consists in the imperturbable belief that, with the clue of logic, thinking can reach to the nethermost depths of being, and that thinking can not only perceive being but even modify it. This sublime metaphysical illusion is added as an instinct to science and again and again leads the latter to its limits, where it must change into *art; which is really the end to be attained by this mechanism.*

If we now look at Socrates in the light of this idea, he appears to us as the first who could not only live, but — what is far greater — also die by the guidance of this instinct of science: and hence the picture of the *dying Socrates*, as the man raised above the fear of death by knowledge and reason, is the sign above the entrance-gate of science reminding every one of its mission, namely, to make existence seem intelligible, and therefore justified: for which purpose, if arguments are not enough, *myth* also must be used, which I have just indicated as the necessary consequence, as the very goal of science.

He who once sees clearly how, after Socrates, the mystagogue of science, one philosophical school succeeds another, like wave upon wave; — how an entirely unforeseen universal development of the thirst for knowledge throughout the cultured world (together with the feeling that the acquisition of knowledge was the specific task of every one highly gifted) led science on to the high sea from which since then it has never been entirely driven. He who sees how through the universality of this movement a common net of thought was for the first time stretched over the entire globe, with prospects, moreover, of conformity to law in an entire solar system; — He who realizes all this, together with the amazingly high pyramid of our contemporary knowledge, cannot fail to see in Socrates the turning-point and vortex of so-called universal history. For if one were to imagine the whole incalculable sum of energy which has been used up by that universal tendency, — used _not_ in the service of knowledge, but for the practical, _i.e._, egotistical ends of individuals and peoples — then probably the instinctive love of life would be so much weakened in general wars of destruction and continual migrations of peoples, that, owing to the practice of suicide, the individual would perhaps feel the last remnant of a sense of duty, similar to that of the Fiji Islander who, as son, strangles his parents and, as friend, his friend: and thus a practical pessimism might even give rise to a horrible ethics of general slaughter out of pity — which, as a matter of fact, exists and has existed wherever art in one form or another, especially as science and religion, has not appeared as a remedy for and preventive of that pestilential breath.

As against this practical pessimism, Socrates is the prototype of the theoretical optimist who with his belief in the explicability of the nature of things, attributes to knowledge and perception the power of a universal panacea, and in error sees evil in itself. To penetrate into the depths and to distinguish true perception from error and illusion seemed to the Socratic man the noblest and even the only truly human calling: just as from the time of Socrates onwards the mechanism of making concepts, judgments, and inferences was prized above all other activities as the highest talent and the most admirable gift of nature. Even the sublimest moral acts, the stirrings of pity, of self-sacrifice, of heroism, and that tranquillity of soul, so difficult of attainment, which the Apollonian Greek called Euphrosyne were, by Socrates, and his like-minded successors up to today, derived from the dialectic of knowledge and accordingly were designated as teachable. Any one who has experienced in himself the joy of a Socratic perception, and felt how, in constantly widening circles, it seeks to embrace the entire world of phenomena, will thenceforth find no stimulus urging him to existence more forcible than the desire to complete that conquest, to draw the net impenetrably close. To such a temper the Platonic Socrates then appears as the teacher of an entirely new form of "Greek cheerfulness" and vital happiness, which seeks to express itself in action, and will, for the most part, find that expression in maieutic and pedagogic influences on noble youths, with a view to the ultimate production of genius.

But now science, stimulated by its powerful illusion, hastens irresistibly to its limits, on which its optimism, hidden in the essence of logic, is wrecked. For the periphery of the circle of science has an infinite number of points, and while there is still no telling how this circle can ever be completely measured, yet the noble and gifted man, even before the middle of his career, inevitably comes in contact with those extreme points of the periphery where he stares into the unfathomable. When to his dismay he here sees how logic coils round itself at these limits and finally bites its own tail — then the new form of perception rises to view, namely *tragic perception*, which, in order even to be endured, requires art as protection and remedy.

With eyes strengthened and refreshed by the sight of the Greeks, let us look upon the highest spheres of the world around us. We behold the eagerness of the insatiate optimistic knowledge, of which Socrates is the typical representative, transformed into tragic resignation and the need for art: while, to be sure, this same avidity, in its lower stages, must exhibit itself as inimical to art, and must especially have an inward detestation of Dionyso-tragic art, as was exemplified in the opposition of Socratism to Æschylean tragedy.

Here then, in a mood of agitation, we knock at the gates of the present and the future: will that "transforming" lead to ever-new configurations of genius, and especially of the *music-practicing* Socrates? Will the net of art which is spread over the whole of existence, whether under the name of religion or of science, be knit ever more closely and delicately, or is it destined to be torn to shreds under the restlessly barbaric activity and whirl which calls itself "the present"? Anxious, yet not despairing, we stand apart for a brief space, like spectators who are permitted to be witnesses of these tremendous struggles and transitions. Alas! It is the magic effect of these struggles that he who beholds them must also participate in them!

16

BY this elaborate historical example we have sought to make it clear that just as surely as tragedy perishes with the evanescence of the spirit of music, so sure is it that only from this spirit can it be reborn. In order to qualify the singularity of this assertion, and, on the other hand, to disclose the origin of this insight, we must now confront clearly the analogous phenomena of our own time; we must enter into the midst of those struggles, which, as I have just said, are being waged in the highest spheres of our contemporary world between the insatiate optimistic perception and the tragic need of art. In my examination I shall leave out of account all those other antagonistic tendencies which at all times oppose art, especially tragedy, and which now are again extending their triumphant sway to such an extent that of the theatrical arts only the farce and the ballet, for example, put forth their blossoms, which perhaps not every one cares to smell, in rather rich luxuriance. I will speak only of the *most noted opposition* to the tragic world-conception — and by this I mean optimistic science in its most essential form with its ancestor Socrates at its head. A little later on I shall also name those forces which seem to me to guarantee a *rebirth of tragedy* — and perhaps other blessed hopes for the German genius!

Before we plunge into the midst of these struggles, let us array ourselves in the armor of the knowledge we have already acquired. In contrast to all those who are intent on deriving the arts from one exclusive principle, as the necessary vital source of every work of art, I shall keep my eyes fixed on the two artistic deities of the Greeks, Apollo and Dionysus, and recognize in them the living and conspicuous representatives of *two* worlds of art differing in their intrinsic essence and in their highest aims. I see Apollo as the transfiguring genius of the *principium individuationis* through which alone the redemption in appearance is truly to be obtained; while by the mystical triumphant cry of Dionysus the spell of individuation is broken, and the way lies open to the Mothers of Being,[17] to the innermost heart of things. This extraordinary antithesis, which stretches like a yawning gulf between plastic art as the Apollonian, and music as the Dionysian art, has revealed itself to only one of the great thinkers, to such an extent that, even without this clue to the symbolism of the Hellenic divinities, he conceded to music a character different from, and an origin anterior to, all the other arts, because, unlike them, it is not a copy of the phenomenon, but an immediate copy of the will itself, and therefore represents *the metaphysical of everything physical in the world*, the thing-in-itself of every phenomenon. (Schopenhauer, *Welt als Wille und Vorstellung*, I. 310.)[18] To this most important perception of esthetics (with which, in the most serious sense, esthetics properly begins), Richard Wagner, by way of confirmation of its eternal truth, affixed his seal, when he asserted in his *Beethoven* that music must be evaluated according to esthetic principles quite different from those which apply to all plastic arts, and not, in general, according to the category of beauty: although an erroneous esthetics, inspired by a mistaken and degenerate art, has, by virtue of the concept of beauty obtaining in the plastic domain, accustomed itself to demand of music an effect similar to that produced by works of plastic art, namely, the arousing of *delight in beautiful forms*. Upon perceiving this extraordinary antithesis, I felt a strong necessity to approach the essence of Greek tragedy and, with it, the profoundest revelation of the

---

[17] Cf. *Faust*, Part 2. Act I.
[18] *World as Will and Idea*, I. p. 338, trans. by Haldane and Kemp, 6th ed.

Hellenic genius: for I at last thought that I possessed a charm to enable me — far beyond the phraseology of our usual esthetics — to represent vividly to my mind the fundamental problem of tragedy: whereby I was granted such a surprising and unusual insight into the Hellenic character that it necessarily seemed to me as if our classical-Hellenic science that bears itself so proudly had thus far contrived to subsist mainly on phantasmagoria and externals.

Perhaps we may lead up to this fundamental problem by asking: what esthetic effect results when the essentially separate art-forces, the Apollonian and the Dionysian, enter into simultaneous activity? Or more briefly: how is music related to image and concept? Schopenhauer, whom Richard Wagner, with special reference to this point, praises for an unsurpassable clearness and perspicuity of exposition, expresses himself most thoroughly on the subject in the following passage which I shall cite here at full length[19] (*Welt als Wille und Vorstellung*, I. p. 309): "According to all this, we may regard the phenomenal world, or nature, and music as two different expressions of the same thing,[20] which is therefore itself the only medium of their analogy, so that a knowledge of it is demanded in order to understand that analogy. Music, therefore, if regarded as an expression of the world, is in the highest degree a universal language, which is related indeed to the universality of concepts, much as they are related to the particular things. Its universality, however, is by no means that empty universality of abstraction, but quite of a different kind, and is united with thorough and distinct definiteness. In this respect it resembles geometrical figures and numbers, which are the universal forms of all possible objects of experience and applicable to them all *a priori*, and yet are not abstract but perceptible and thoroughly determinate. All possible efforts, excitements and manifestations of will, all that goes on in the heart of man and that reason includes in the wide, negative concept of feeling, may be expressed by the infinite number of possible melodies, but always in the universal, in the mere form, without the material, always according to the thing-in-itself, not the phenomenon, the inmost soul, as it were, of the phenomenon without the body. This deep relation which music has to the true nature of all things also explains the fact that suitable music played to any scene, action, event, or surrounding seems to disclose to us its most secret meaning, and appears as the most accurate and distinct commentary upon it. This is so truly the case, that whoever gives himself up entirely to the impression of a symphony, seems to see all the possible

---

[19] *World as Will and Idea*, I. p. 239 —, trans. by Haldane and Kemp, 6th ed.
[20] That is, "the will" as understood by Schopenhauer.

events of life and the world take place in himself, yet if he reflects, he can find no likeness between the music and the things that passed before his mind. For, as we have said, music is distinguished from all the other arts by the fact that it is not a copy of the phenomenon, or, more accurately, the adequate objectivity of the will, but is the direct copy of the will itself, and therefore exhibits itself as the metaphysical to everything physical in the world, and as the thing-in-itself to every phenomenon. We might, therefore, just as well call the world embodied music as embodied will; and this is the reason why music makes every picture, and indeed every scene of real life and of the world, at once appear with higher significance, certainly all the more, in proportion as its melody is analogous to the inner spirit of the given phenomenon. It rests upon this that we are able to set a poem to music as a song, or a perceptible representation as a pantomime, or both as an opera. Such particular pictures of human life, set to the universal language of music, are never bound to it or correspond to it with stringent necessity; but they stand to it only in the relation of an example chosen at will to a general concept. In the determinateness of the real, they represent that which music expresses in the universality of mere form. For melodies are to a certain extent, like general concepts, an abstraction from the actual. This actual world, then, the world of particular things, affords the object of perception, the special and individual, the particular case, both to the universality of the concepts and to the universality of the melodies. But these two universalities are in a certain respect opposed to each other; for the concepts contain particulars only as the first forms abstracted from perception, as it were, the separated shell of things; thus they are, strictly speaking, *abstracta:* music, on the other hand, gives the inmost kernel which precedes all forms, or the heart of things. This relation may be very well expressed in the language of the schoolmen, by saying, the concepts are the *universalia post rem,* but music gives the *universalia ante rem,* and the real world the *universalia in re.* But that in general a relation is possible between a composition and a perceptible representation rests, as we have said, upon the fact that both are simply different expressions of the same inner being of the world. When now, in the particular case, such a relation is actually given, that is to say, when the composer has been able to express in the universal language of music the emotions of will which constitute the heart of an event, then the melody of the song, the music of the opera, is expressive. But the analogy discovered by the composer between the two must have proceeded from the direct knowledge of the nature of the world unknown to his reason, and must not be an imitation produced with conscious intention by means of conceptions, otherwise the music does not express the inner nature of the will itself, but merely gives an inadequate imitation of its phenomenon. All specially imitative music does this."

According to the doctrine of Schopenhauer, therefore, we may understand music as the immediate language of the will, and we feel our fancy stimulated to give form to this invisible and yet so actively stirred spirit-world which speaks to us, and we feel prompted to embody it in an analogous example. On the other hand, image and concept, under the influence of a truly corresponding music, acquire a higher significance. Dionysian art therefore is wont to exercise two kinds of influences on the Apollonian art-faculty: music incites to the *symbolic-intuition* of Dionysian universality, and music allows the symbolic image to emerge *in its highest significance*. From these facts, intelligible in themselves and not inaccessible to a more penetrating examination, I infer the capacity of music to give birth to *myth* (the most significant exemplar), and particularly the *tragic* myth: the myth which expresses Dionysian knowledge in symbols. In the phenomenon of the lyrist, I have shown how music strives to express its nature in Apollonian images. If now we reflect that music at its greatest intensity must seek to attain also to its highest symbolization, we must deem it possible that it also knows how to find the symbolic expression for its unique Dionysian wisdom; and where shall we seek for this expression if not in tragedy and, in general, in the conception of the tragic?

From the nature of art as it is usually conceived according to the single category of appearance and beauty, the tragic cannot honestly be deduced at all; it is only through the spirit of music that we can understand the joy involved in the annihilation of the individual. For only by the particular examples of such annihilation are we made clear as to the eternal phenomenon of Dionysian art, which gives expression to the will in its omnipotence, as it were, behind the *principium individuationis*, the eternal life beyond all phenomena, and despite all annihilation. The metaphysical joy in the tragic is a translation of the instinctive unconscious Dionysian wisdom into the language of the scene: the hero, the highest manifestation of the will, is disavowed for our pleasure, because he is only phenomenon, and because the eternal life of the will is not affected by his annihilation. "We believe in eternal life," exclaims tragedy; while music is the immediate idea of this life. Plastic art has an altogether different aim: here Apollo dispels the suffering of the individual by the radiant glorification of the *eternity of the phenomenon*: here beauty triumphs over the suffering inherent in life; pain is in a sense obliterated from the features of nature. In Dionysian art and its tragic symbolism the same nature cries to us with its true, undissembled voice: "Be as I am! Amidst the ceaseless flux of phenomena I am the eternally creative primordial mother, eternally impelling to existence, eternally self-sufficient amid this flux of phenomena!"

17

DIONYSIAN art, too, wishes to convince us of the eternal joy of existence: only we are to seek this joy not in phenomena, but behind them. We are to recognize that all that comes into being must be ready for a sorrowful end; we are forced to look into the terrors of the individual existence — yet we are not to become rigid with fear: a metaphysical comfort tears us momentarily from the bustle of the transforming figures. We are really for a brief moment Primordial Being itself, feeling its raging desire for existence and joy in existence; the struggle, the pain, the destruction of phenomena, now appear to us as a necessary thing, in view of the surplus of countless forms of existence which force and push one another into life, in view of the exuberant fertility of the universal will. We are pierced by the maddening sting of these pains just when we have become, as it were, one with the infinite primordial joy in existence, and when we anticipate, in Dionysian ecstasy, the indestructibility and eternity of this joy. In spite of fear and pity, we are the happy living beings, not as individuals, but as the *one* living being, with whose creative joy we are united.

The history of the rise of Greek tragedy now tells us with luminous precision that the tragic art of the Greeks was really born of the spirit of music, with which conception we believe we have done justice for the first time to the primitive and astonishing significance of the chorus. At the same time, however, we must admit that the meaning of tragic myth set forth above never became clearly apparent to the Greek poets, not to speak of the Greek philosophers; their heroes speak, as it were, more superficially than they act; the myth does not at all obtain adequate objectification in the spoken word. The structure of the scenes and the intuitively created images reveal a deeper wisdom than the poet himself can put into words and concepts: the same is also observable in Shakespeare, whose Hamlet, for instance, similarly, talks more superficially than he acts, so that the previously mentioned lesson of Hamlet is to be deduced, not from his words, but from a profound contemplation and survey of the whole. With respect to Greek tragedy, which of course presents itself to us only as word-drama, I have even intimated that the lack of congruity between myth and expression might easily lead us to regard it as shallower and less significant than it really is, and accordingly to predicate for it a more superficial effect than it must have had according to the testimony of the ancients: for how easily one forgets that what the word-poet did not succeed in doing, namely, to attain the highest spiritualization and ideality of the myth, he might very well succeed in doing every moment as creative musician! To be sure, we are forced to construct for ourselves by scholarly research the superior power of the musical effect in order to experience something of the incomparable comfort which must have been characteristic of true tragedy. Even this musical superiority, however, would only have been felt by us had we been Greeks: for in the entire development of Greek music — as compared with the infinitely richer music known and familiar to us — we imagine we hear only the youthful song of the musical genius modestly intoned. The Greeks, as the Egyptian priests say, are eternal children, and in tragic art too they are only children who do not know what a sublime plaything has originated in their hands and — is being demolished.

That striving of the spirit of music towards symbolic and mythical objectification, which increases from the beginnings of lyric poetry up to Attic tragedy, suddenly breaks off immediately after attaining a luxuriant development, and disappears, as it were, from the surface of Hellenic art: while the Dionysian world-view born of this striving lives on in the Mysteries and, in its strangest metamorphoses and debasements, does not cease to attract serious natures. Will it not some day rise once again out of its mystic depths as art?

Here we are detained by the question, whether the power, by virtue of whose opposing influence tragedy perished, has for all time sufficient strength to prevent the artistic reawakening of tragedy and the tragic world-view. If ancient tragedy was diverted from its course by the dialectical desire for knowledge and the optimism of science, this fact might lead us to believe that there is an eternal conflict between *the theoretic* and *the tragic world-view*; and only after the spirit of science has been pursued to its limits, and its claim to universal validity destroyed by the evidence of these limits may we hope for a rebirth of tragedy: for which form of culture we should have to use the symbol *of the music-practicing Socrates* in the sense spoken of above. In this contrast, I understand by the spirit of science the belief which first came to light in the person of Socrates — the belief in the explicability of nature and in knowledge as a panacea.

He who recalls the immediate consequences of this restless urgent spirit of science will realize at once that *myth* was annihilated by it, and that, because of this annihilation, poetry was driven like a homeless being from her natural ideal soil. If we have been right in assigning to music the power of reproducing myth from itself, we may similarly expect to find the spirit of science on the path where it inimically opposes this mythopœic power of music. This takes place in the development of the *New Attic Dithyramb*, the music of which no longer expressed the inner essence, the will itself, but only rendered the phenomenon approximately, in an imitation by means of concepts; from which intrinsically degenerate music the genuinely musical natures turned away with the same repugnance that they felt for the art-destroying tendency of Socrates. The unerring instinct of Aristophanes was surely right when it included Socrates himself, the tragedy of Euripides, and the music of the New Dithyrambic poets in the same feeling of hatred, recognizing in all three phenomena the signs of a degenerate culture. In this New Dithyramb, music is outrageously manipulated so as to be the imitative portrait of a phenomenon, for instance, of a battle or a storm at sea; and thus, of course, it has been utterly robbed of its mythopœic power. For it seeks to arouse pleasure only by impelling us to seek external analogies between a vital or natural process and certain rhythmical figures and characteristic sounds of music; if our understanding is to content itself with the perception of these analogies, we are reduced to a frame of mind which makes impossible any reception of the mythical; for the myth as a unique type of universality and truth towering into the infinite cries to be conspicuously recognized. The truly Dionysian music presents itself as such a general mirror of the universal will: the conspicuous event refracted in this mirror expands at once for our consciousness to the copy of an external truth. Conversely, such a conspicuous event is at once divested of every mythical character by the tone-painting of the New Dithyramb; music now becomes a wretched copy of the phenomenon, and therefore infinitely poorer than the phenomenon itself: through which poverty it still further reduces the phenomenon for our consciousness, so that now, for example, a musically imitated battle of this sort exhausts itself in marches, signal-sounds, etc., and our imagination is arrested precisely by these superficialities. Tone-painting is thus in every respect the antithesis of true music with its mythopœic power: through it the phenomenon, poor in itself, is made still poorer, while through Dionysian music the individual phenomenon is enriched and expanded into a picture of the world. It was a great triumph for the un-Dionysian spirit, when by the development of the New Dithyramb, it had estranged music from itself and reduced it to be the slave of phenomena. Euripides, who, though in a higher sense, must be considered a thoroughly unmusical nature, is for this very reason a passionate adherent of the New Dithyrambic Music, and with the liberality of a freebooter makes use of all its effective tricks and mannerisms.

In another direction also we see at work the power of this un-Dionysian myth-opposing spirit, when we turn our attention to the prevalence of *character representation* and psychological refinement in tragedy from Sophocles onwards. The character must no longer be expanded into an eternal type, but, on the contrary, must develop individually through artistic subordinate traits and shadings, through the nicest precision of all lines, in such a manner that the spectator is in general no longer conscious of the myth, but of the vigorous truth to nature and the artist's imitative power. Here also we observe the victory of the phenomenon over the Universal, and the delight in a unique, almost anatomical preparation; we are already in the atmosphere of a theoretical world, where scientific knowledge is valued more highly than the artistic reflection of a universal law. The movement in the direction of character delineation proceeds rapidly: while Sophocles still portrays complete characters and employs myth for their refined development, Euripides already draws only prominent individual traits of character, which can express themselves in violent bursts of passion; in the New Attic Comedy, however, there are only masks with *one* expression: frivolous old men, duped panders, and cunning slaves, recurring incessantly. Where now is the mythopœic spirit of music? What still remains of music is either excitatory music or associational music, that is, either a stimulant for dull and faded nerves, or tone-painting. As regards the former, it hardly matters about the text set to it: the heroes and choruses of Euripides are already dissolute enough when once they begin to sing; to what pass must things have come with his impertinent successors?

The new un-Dionysian spirit, however, reveals itself most plainly in the *dénouements* of the new dramas. In the Old Tragedy one could sense at the end that metaphysical comfort, without which the delight in tragedy cannot be explained at all; the reconciliating tones from another world sound purest, perhaps, in the *Œdipus at Colonus*. Now that the genius of music has fled from tragedy, tragedy, strictly speaking, is dead: for from what source shall we now draw this metaphysical comfort? The new spirit, therefore, sought for an earthly resolution of the tragic dissonance. The hero, after being sufficiently tortured by fate, earned a well-deserved reward through a splendid marriage or tokens of divine favor. The hero had turned gladiator. On him, after he had been nicely beaten and covered with wounds, freedom was occasionally bestowed. The *deus ex machina* took the place of metaphysical comfort. I will not say that the tragic world-view was everywhere completely destroyed by this intruding un-Dionysian spirit: we only know that it had to flee from art into the underworld as it were, in the degenerate form of a secret cult.

Over the widest extent of the Hellenic character, however, there raged the consuming blast of this spirit, which manifests itself in the form of "Greek cheerfulness," which we have already spoken of as a senile, unproductive love of existence. This cheerfulness is the antithesis of the splendid "naïveté" of the earlier Greeks, which, according to the characteristic indicated above, must be conceived as the blossom of the Apollonian culture springing from a dark abyss, as the victory which the Hellenic will, through its mirroring of beauty, obtains over suffering and the wisdom of suffering. The noblest manifestation of that other form of "Greek cheerfulness," the Alexandrian, is the cheerfulness of the *theoretical man:* it exhibits the same characteristic symptoms that distinguished the spirit of the un-Dionysian: it combats Dionysian wisdom and art, it seeks to dissolve myth, it substitutes for a metaphysical comfort an earthly consonance, in fact, a *deus ex machina* of its own, the god of machines and crucibles, that is, the powers of the forces of nature recognized and employed in the service of the higher egoism; it believes that it can correct the world by knowledge, guide life by science, and actually confine the individual within a limited sphere of solvable problems, from which he can cheerfully say to life: "I desire thee: it is worth while to know thee."

18

IT is an eternal phenomenon: the insatiate will can always, by means of an illusion spread over things, detain its creatures in life and compel them to live on. One is chained by the Socratic love of knowledge and the delusion of being able thereby to heal the eternal wound of existence; another is ensnared by art's seductive veil of beauty fluttering before his eyes; still another by the metaphysical comfort that beneath the flux of phenomena eternal life flows on indestructibly: to say nothing of the more ordinary and almost more powerful illusions which the will has always at hand. These three planes of illusion are on the whole designed only for the more nobly formed natures, who in general feel profoundly the weight and burden of existence, and must be deluded by exquisite stimulants into forgetfulness of their sorrow. All that we call culture is made up of these stimulants; and, according to the proportion of the ingredients, we have either a dominantly *Socratic* or *artistic* or *tragic* culture: or, if historical exemplifications are wanted, there is either an Alexandrian or a Hellenic or a Buddhistic culture.

Our whole modern world is entangled in the net of Alexandrian culture. It proposes as its ideal the theoretical man equipped with the greatest forces of knowledge, and laboring in the service of science, whose archetype and progenitor is Socrates. All our educational methods have originally this ideal in view: every other form of existence must struggle on wearisomely beside it, as something tolerated, but not intended. In an almost alarming manner the cultured man was for a long time found only in the form of the scholar: even our poetical arts have been forced to evolve from learned imitations, and in the main effect, that of rhyme, we still recognize the origin of our poetic form from artistic experiments with a non-indigenous, thoroughly learned language. How unintelligible must *Faust*, the modern cultured man, who is in himself intelligible, have appeared to a true Greek — Faust, storming unsatisfied through all the faculties, devoted to magic and the devil from a desire for knowledge; Faust, whom we have but to place beside Socrates for the purpose of comparison, in order to see that modern man is beginning to divine the limits of this Socratic love of perception and yearns for a coast in the wide waste of the ocean of knowledge. When Goethe on one occasion said to Eckermann with reference to Napoleon: "Yes, my good friend, there is also a productiveness of deeds," he reminded us in a charmingly naïve manner that the non-theorist is something incredible and astounding to modern man; so that we again have need of the wisdom of Goethe to discover that such a surprising form of existence is not only comprehensible, but even pardonable.

Now, we must not hide from ourselves what is concealed at the heart of this Socratic culture: Optimism, with its delusion of limitless power! Well, we must not be alarmed if the fruits of this optimism ripen — if society, leavened to the very lowest strata by this kind of culture, gradually begins to tremble with wanton agitations and desires, if the belief in the earthly happiness of all, if the belief in the possibility of such a general intellectual culture is gradually transformed into the threatening demand for such an Alexandrian earthly happiness, into the conjuring up of a Euripidean *deus ex machina*. Let us mark this well: the Alexandrian culture, to be able to exist permanently, requires a slave class, but, with its optimistic view of life, it denies the necessity of such a class, and consequently, when the effect of its beautifully seductive and tranquillizing utterances about the "dignity of man" and the "dignity of labor" is over, it gradually drifts towards a dreadful destruction. There is nothing more terrible than a barbaric slave class, who have learned to regard their existence as an injustice, and now prepare to avenge, not only themselves, but all future generations. In the face of such threatening storms, who dares to appeal with any confidence to our pale and exhausted religions, whose very foundations have degenerated into "learned" religions? — so that myth, the necessary prerequisite of every religion, is already paralyzed everywhere, and even in this domain the optimistic spirit — which we have just designated as the destroying germ of society — has attained the mastery.

While the evil slumbering in the heart of theoretical culture gradually begins to disquiet modern man, while he anxiously ransacks the stores of his experience for means to avert the danger, though he has no great faith in these means; while he, therefore, begins to divine the consequences of his position: great, universally gifted natures have contrived, with an incredible amount of thought, to make use of the paraphernalia of science itself, in order to point out the limits and the relativity of knowledge generally, and thus definitely to deny the claim of science to universal validity and universal aims: with which demonstration the illusory notion was for the first time recognized as such, which pretends, with the aid of causality, to be able to fathom the innermost essence of things. The extraordinary courage and wisdom of *Kant* and *Schopenhauer* have succeeded in gaining the most difficult victory, the victory over the optimism hidden in the essence of logic, which optimism in turn is the basis of our culture. While this optimism, resting on apparently unobjectionable *æternæ veritates*, had believed in the intelligibility and solvability of all the riddles of the universe, and had treated space, time, and causality as totally unconditioned laws of the most universal validity, Kant, on the other hand, showed that in reality these served only to elevate the mere phenomenon, the work of Mâyâ, to the position of the sole and highest reality, putting it in place of the innermost and true essence of things, and thus making impossible any knowledge of this essence or, in Schopenhauer's words, lulling the dreamer still more soundly asleep. With this knowledge a culture is inaugurated which I venture to call a tragic culture; the most important characteristic of which is that wisdom takes the place of science as the highest end, wisdom, which, uninfluenced by the seductive distractions of the sciences, turns with unmoved eye to a comprehensive view of the world, and seeks to conceive therein, with sympathetic feelings of love, the eternal suffering as its own. Let us imagine a rising generation with this bold vision, this heroic desire for the magnificent, let us imagine the valiant step of these dragon-slayers, the proud daring with which they turn their backs on all the effeminate doctrines of optimism that they may "live resolutely," wholly, and fully: would it not be necessary for the tragic man of this culture, with his self-discipline of seriousness and terror, to desire a new art, the art of metaphysical comfort — namely, tragedy — to claim it as Helen, and exclaim with Faust:

"Und sollt' ich nicht, sehnsüchtigster Gewalt,
Ins Leben ziehn die einzigste Gestalt?"[21]

But now that the Socratic culture can only hold the scepter of its infallibility with trembling hands; now that it has been shaken from two directions — once by the fear of its own conclusions which it at length begins to surmise, and again, because it no longer has its former naïve confidence in the eternal validity of its foundation — it is a sad spectacle to see how the dance of its thought rushes longingly on ever-new forms, to embrace them, and then, shuddering, lets them go suddenly as Mephistopheles does the seductive Lamiæ. It is certainly the sign of the "breach" which all are wont to speak of as the fundamental tragedy of modern culture that the theoretical man, alarmed and dissatisfied at his own conclusions, no longer dares entrust himself to the terrible ice-stream of existence: he runs timidly up and down the bank. So thoroughly has he been spoiled by his optimistic views that he no longer wants to have anything whole, with all of nature's cruelty attaching to it. Besides, he feels that a culture based on the principles of science must be destroyed when it begins to grow *illogical*, that is, to retreat before its own conclusions. Our art reveals this universal trouble: in vain does one depend imitatively on all the great productive periods and natures; in vain does one accumulate the entire "World-literature" around modern man for his comfort; in vain does one place one's self in the midst of the art-styles and artists of all ages, so that one may give names to them as Adam did to the beasts: one still continues eternally hungry, the "critic" without joy and energy, the Alexandrian man, who is at bottom a librarian and corrector of proofs, and who, pitiable wretch, goes blind from the dusty books and printers' errors.

19

WE cannot indicate the essential modern content of this Socratic culture more distinctly than by calling it *the culture of the opera*: for it is in this department that this culture has expressed its aims and perceptions, with special naïveté, which is surprising when we compare the genesis of the opera and the facts of operatic development with the eternal truths of the Apollonian and Dionysian. I call to mind first of all the

---

[21] And shall not I, by mightiest desire, In living shape that sole fair form acquire? *Faust*, Swanwick's trans.

origin of the *stile rappresentativo* and the recitative. Is it credible that this thoroughly externalized undevotional operatic music, could be received and cherished with enthusiastic favor, as a rebirth, as it were, of all true music, by the very age in which had appeared the ineffably sublime and sacred music of Palestrina? And who, on the other hand, would think of making only the diversion-craving luxuriousness of those Florentine circles and the vanity of their dramatic singers responsible for the love of the opera which spread with such rapidity? That in the same age, even among the same people, this passion for a half-musical mode of speech should awaken alongside of the vaulted structure of Palestrina harmonies which all medieval Christendom had been building up, I can explain to myself only by a co-operating, *extra-artistic tendency* in the essence of the recitative.

The listener, who insists on distinctly hearing the words under the music, has his desire fulfilled by the singer in that the latter speaks rather than sings, and by this half-song intensifies the pathetic expression of the words. By this intensification of the pathos he facilitates the understanding of the words and surmounts the remaining half of the music. The specific danger now threatening him is that in some unguarded moment he may stress the music unduly, which would immediately entail the destruction of the pathos of the speech and the distinctness of the words: while, on the other hand, he feels himself continually impelled to musical delivery and to a virtuose exhibition of vocal talent. Here the "poet" comes to his aid, who knows how to provide him with abundant opportunities for lyrical interjections, repetitions of words and sentences, etc. — at which places the singer, now in the purely musical element, can rest himself without paying any attention to the words. This alternation of emotionally impressive speech which, however, is only half sung, with interjections which are wholly sung, an alternation characteristic of the *stile rappresentativo*, this rapidly changing endeavor to affect now the conceptional and representative faculty of the hearer, now his musical sense, is something so utterly unnatural and likewise so intrinsically contradictory both to the Apollonian and Dionysian artistic impulses, that one has to infer an origin of the recitative lying outside all artistic instincts. According to this description, the recitative must be defined as a mixture of epic and lyric delivery, not indeed as an intrinsically stable mixture, a state not to be attained in the case of such totally disparate elements, but as an entirely superficial mosaic conglutination, such as is totally unprecedented in the domain of nature and experience. *But this was not the opinion of the inventors of the recitative:* they themselves, together with their age, believed rather that the mystery of antique music has been solved by this *stile rappresentativo*, in which, so they thought, was to be found the only explanation of the enormous influence of an Orpheus, an Amphion, and even of Greek tragedy. The new style was looked upon as the reawakening of the most effective music, the Old Greek music: indeed, in accordance with the universal and popular conception of the Homeric *as the primitive world*, they could abandon themselves to the dream of having descended once more into the para-disiacal beginnings of mankind, where music also must have had that unsurpassed purity, power, and innocence of which the poets, in their pastoral plays, could give such touching accounts. Here we can see into the internal development of this thoroughly modern variety of art, the opera: art here responds to a powerful need, but it is a need of the belief in the prehistoric existence of the artistic, of an unesthetic kind: the longing for the idyllic, good man. The recitative was regarded as the rediscovered language of this primitive man; the opera as the found country of this idyllically or heroically good creature, who simultaneously with every action follows a natural artistic impulse, who accomplishes his speech with a little singing, in order that he may immediately break forth into full song at the slightest emotional excitement. It is now a matter of indif-ference to us that the humanists of the time combated the old ecclesiasti-cal conception of man as inherently corrupt and lost, with this newly created picture of the paradisiacal artist: so that opera is to be understood as the opposition dogma of the good man, but may also, at the same time, provide a consolation for that pessimism which, owing to the frightful uncertainty of all conditions of life, attracted precisely the serious-minded men of the time. For us, it is enough to have perceived that the essential charm, and therefore the genesis, of this new art-life lies in the gratification of an altogether unesthetic need, in the optimistic glorifica-tion of man as such, in the conception of the primitive man as the man naturally good and artistic: a principle of the opera that has gradually changed into a threatening and terrible *demand*, which, in face of con-temporary socialistic movements, we can no longer ignore. The "good primitive man" wants his rights: what paradisiacal prospects! Beside this I place another equally obvious confirmation of my view that opera is based on the same principles as our Alexandrian culture. Opera is the birth of the theoretical man, the critical layman, not of the artist: one of the most surprising facts in the whole history of art. It was the demand of thoroughly unmusical hearers that before everything else the words must be understood, so that according to them a rebirth of music is to be ex-pected only when some mode of singing has been discovered in which text-word lords over counterpoint like master over servant. For the words, it is argued, are as much nobler than the accompanying harmonic system as the soul is nobler than the body. It was in accordance with the laically unmusical crudeness of these views that the combination of music, picture and words was effected in the beginnings of the opera: and in the spirit of this esthetic the first experiments were made in the leading amateur circles of Florence by the poets and singers patronized there. The man incapable of art creates for himself a kind of art precisely because he is the inartistic man as such. Because he cannot divine the Dionysian depth of music, he changes his musical taste into an appreciation of the understandable word-and-tone-rhetoric of the passions in the *stile rappresentativo*, and into the voluptuousness of the lyric arts; because he is unable to behold a vision, he forces the machinist and the decorative artist into his service; because he cannot comprehend the true nature of the artist, he conjures up the "artistic primitive man" to suit his taste, that is, the man who sings and recites verses under the influence of passion. He dreams himself back into a time when passion sufficed to generate songs and poems: as if emotion had ever been able to create anything artistic. The premise of the opera is a false belief concerning the artistic process, in fact, the idyllic belief that every sentient man is an artist. This belief would make opera the expression of the taste of the laity in art, dictating their laws with the cheerful optimism of the theoretical man.

Should we desire to combine the two conceptions just set forth as influential in the origin of opera, it would merely remain for us to speak of an *idyllic tendency of the opera:* in which connection we may avail ourselves exclusively of the phraseology and illustration of Schiller. "Nature and the ideal," he says, "are either objects of grief, when the former is represented as lost, the latter unattained; or both are objects of joy, in that they are represented as real. The first case furnishes the elegy in its narrower signification, the second the idyll in its widest sense." Here we must at once call attention to the common characteristic of these two conceptions in the genesis of opera, namely, that in them the ideal is not felt as unattained or nature as lost. In consonance with this sentiment, there was a primitive age of man when he lay close to the heart of nature, and, owing to this naturalness, had at once attained the ideal of mankind in a paradisiacal goodness and artistry. From this perfect primitive man all of us were supposed to be descended. We were, in fact, faithful copies of him; only we had to cast off some few things in order to recognize ourselves once more as this primitive man, on the strength of a voluntary renunciation of superfluous learnedness, of superabundant culture. It was to such a concord of nature and the ideal, to an idyllic reality, that the cultured Renaissance man let himself be led back by his operatic imitation of Greek tragedy. He made use of this tragedy as Dante made use of Vergil, in order to be conducted to the gates of paradise: while from this point he continued unassisted and passed over from an imitation of the highest Greek art-form to a "restoration of all things," to an imitation of man's original art-world. What a cheerful confidence there is about these daring endeavors, in the very heart of theoretical culture! — solely to be explained by the comforting belief, that "man-in-himself" is the eternally virtuous hero of the opera, the eternally fluting or singing shepherd, who must always in the end rediscover himself as such should he ever at any time have really lost himself; to be considered solely as the fruit of that optimism, which here rises like a sweetishly seductive column of vapor out of the death of the Socratic world-view.

Therefore, the features of the opera do not in any sense exhibit the elegiac sorrow of an eternal loss, but rather the cheerfulness of eternal rediscovery, the indolent delight in an idyllic reality which one can at least momentarily imagine as real. But in this process one may some day grasp the fact that this supposed reality is nothing but a fantastically silly dawdling, at which every one who could judge it by the terrible serious-ness of true nature, and compare it with actual primitive scenes of the beginnings of mankind, would be impelled to call out with loathing: Away with the phantom! Nevertheless, it would be a mistake to imagine that it is possible merely by a vigorous shout to frighten away such a dawdling thing as the opera, as if it were a specter. He who would destroy the opera must take up the struggle against Alexandrian cheerfulness, which expresses itself so naïvely therein concerning its favorite concep-tions; of which in fact it is the specific form of art. But what may art itself expect from the operation of an art-form whose beginnings lie entirely outside of the esthetic province? Which has rather stolen over from a half-moral sphere into the artistic domain, and has been able only occasionally to deceive us as to its hybrid origin? By what sap is this parasitic operatic-form nourished, if not by that of true art? Must we not suppose that the highest and, indeed, the truly serious task of art, — to release the eye from its gaze into the horrors of night and to deliver the "patient" by the healing balm of appearance from the spasms of the agitations of the will, — must we not suppose that this task will degener-ate under the influence of its idyllic seductions and Alexandrian adula-tion to an empty and dissipating dilettanteism? What will become of the eternal truths of the Dionysian and Apollonian in such a *mélange de genres*, as I have shown to be the essence of the *stile rappresentativo*? A style in which music is regarded as the servant, the text as the master, where music is compared with the body, the text with the soul? where at best the highest aim will be directed toward a paraphrastic tone-painting, just as formerly in the New Attic Dithyramb? where music is completely alienated from its true dignity of being the Dionysian mirror of the world, so that the only thing left to it, as the slave of phenomena, is to imitate the formal character of phenomena, and to arouse a superficial pleasure in the play of lines and proportions. Closely observed, this fatal influence of the opera on music is seen to coincide exactly with the universal development of modern music; the optimism lurking in the genesis of the opera and in the character of the culture thereby represented, has, with alarming rapidity, succeeded in divesting music of its Dionyso-cosmic mission and impressing on it a playfully formal and pleasurable character: a change to which the only analogy perhaps is the metamorphosis of the Æschylean man into the cheerful Alexandrian.

If, however, in the exemplification here indicated, we have rightly associated the disappearance of the Dionysian spirit with a most striking, but hitherto unexplained, transformation and degeneration of the Hellenic man — what hopes must revive in us when the most certain auspices guarantee *the reverse process, the gradual awakening of the Dionysian spirit* in our modern world! It is impossible that the divine strength of Heracles should languish for ever in voluptuous bondage to Omphale. Out of the Dionysian root of the German spirit a power has arisen which, having nothing in common with the primitive conditions of Socratic culture, can neither be explained nor excused by it, but which is rather felt by this culture as something terribly inexplicable and overwhelmingly hostile. I refer, of course, to *German music* as we must understand it, particularly in its vast solar orbit from Bach to Beethoven, from Beethoven to Wagner. Even under the most favorable circumstances what can the knowledge-craving Socratism of our days do with this demon rising from unfathomable depths? Neither by means of the zigzag and arabesque work of operatic melody, nor with the aid of the arithmetical counting-board of fugue and contrapuntal dialectic is the formula to be found, by whose thrice-powerful light one might subdue this demon and compel it to speak. What a spectacle, when our latter-day estheticians, with a net of "beauty" peculiar to themselves, pursue and clutch at the genius of music whirling before display activities which are not to be judged by the standard of eternal beauty any more than by the standard of the sublime. Let us but observe these patrons of music at close range, as they really are, indefatigably crying: "Beauty! beauty!" We may discover whether they really bear the stamp of nature's darling children who are fostered and nourished at the breast of the beautiful, or whether they are not rather seeking a deceptive cloak for their own rudeness, an esthetical pretext for their own impassive insipidity: I am thinking here, for instance, of Otto Jahn. But let the liar and the hypocrite beware of our German music: for amid all our culture it is really the only genuine, pure and purifying fire-spirit from which and towards which, as in the teaching of the great Heraclitus of Ephesus, all things move in a double orbit: all that we now call culture, education, civilization, must some day appear before the unerring judge, Dionysus.

Let us recollect further that Kant and Schopenhauer made it possible for the spirit of *German philosophy*, streaming from similar sources, to destroy scientific Socratism's complacent delight in existence by establishing its boundaries; how through this delimitation was introduced an infinitely profounder and more serious view of ethical problems and of art, which we may unhesitatingly designate as Dionysian wisdom comprised in concepts. To what then does the mystery of this oneness of German music and philosophy point if not to a new form of existence, concerning whose character we can only inform ourselves by surmise from Hellenic analogies? For to us who stand on the boundary line between two different forms of existence, the Hellenic prototype retains this immeasurable value, that therein all these transitions and struggles are imprinted in a classically instructive form: except that we, as it were, pass through the chief epochs of the Hellenic genius, analogically in *reverse* order, and seem now, for instance, to be passing backwards from the Alexandrian age to the period of tragedy. At the same time we have the feeling that the birth of a tragic age simply means a return to itself of the German spirit, a blessed self-rediscovery after powerful intrusive influences had for a long time compelled it, living as it did in a helpless and unchaste barbarism, to servitude under their form. Now at last, upon returning to the primitive source of its being, it may venture to stride along boldly and freely before the eyes of all nations without being attached to the leading-strings of a Romanic civilization: if only it can learn implicitly from one people — the Greeks, from whom to learn at all is itself a high honor and a rare distinction. And when were we in greater need of these highest of all teachers more than at present, when we are experiencing a *rebirth of tragedy* and are in danger alike of not knowing whence it comes and of being unable to make clear to ourselves whither it tends?

20

SOME day before an impartial judge, it may be decided in what time and in what men the German spirit has thus far striven most resolutely to learn from the Greeks: and if we confidently assume that this unique praise must be accorded to the noblest intellectual efforts of Goethe, Schiller, and Winkelmann, we will certainly be compelled to add that since their time and subsequent to the more immediate consequences of their efforts, the endeavor to attain to culture and to the Greeks by a similar path has grown incomprehensibly feebler and feebler. That we may not despair utterly of the German spirit, must we not conclude that possibly, in some essential matter, even these champions could not penetrate into the core of the Hellenic nature, and were unable to establish a permanent alliance between German and Greek culture? So that perhaps an unconscious perception of this shortcoming might arouse also in more serious minds the disheartening doubt as to whether after such predecessors they could advance still farther on this path of culture, or could reach the goal at all. Accordingly, since that time, we see that opinions concerning the value of Greek contributions to culture have been degenerating in the most alarming manner; the expression of compassionate superiority may be heard in the most varied intellectual and non-intellectual camps; or elsewhere a totally impotent rhetoric plays with the phrases "Greek harmony," "Greek beauty," "Greek cheerfulness." And in those very circles whose dignified task it might be to draw indefatigably from the Greek reservoir for the good of German culture, in the teaching circles of the higher educational institutions, they have learned best to compromise with the Greeks easily and in good time, often to the extent of a skeptical abandonment of the Hellenic ideal and a total perversion of the true purpose of antiquarian studies. If there is any one at all in these circles who has not completely exhausted himself in his endeavor to be a dependable corrector of old texts or a natural-history microscopist of language, he perhaps is also seeking to take over Grecian antiquity "historically" along with other antiquities, and in any case according to the method and with the supercilious air of our present cultured historiography. Therefore, when the intrinsic efficiency of our higher educational institutions has perhaps never been lower or feebler than at present; when the "journalist," the paper slave of the day, triumphs over the professor in all matters pertaining to culture; and when there remains to the latter only the often previously experienced metamorphosis of now fluttering also like a cheerful cultured butterfly (to use the idiom of the journalist), with the "light elegance" peculiar to this sphere; — under these conditions, with what a painful confusion must the cultured persons of a period like the present gaze at the phenomenon which perhaps is to be comprehended analogically only by means of the profoundest principle of the hitherto unintelligible Hellenic genius, the phenomenon of the reawakening of the Dionysian spirit and the rebirth of tragedy. There has never been another art-period in which so-called culture and true art have been so estranged and opposed, as we may observe them to be at present. We can understand why so feeble a culture hates true art; it fears destruction from its hands. But must not an entire cultural-form, namely, the

Socratic-Alexandrian, have exhausted itself after culminating in such a daintily tapering point as our present culture? If heroes like Goethe and Schiller could not succeed in breaking open the enchanted gate which leads into the Hellenic magic mountain; if with their most dauntless striving they could not go beyond the longing gaze which Goethe's Iphigenia casts from barbaric Tauris to her home across the ocean, what could the epigones of such heroes hope for? — unless the gate — amidst the mystic tones of reawakened tragic music — should open for them suddenly of its own accord, from an entirely different side, quite over-looked in all previous cultural endeavors.

Let no one attempt to trouble our faith in an impending rebirth of Hellenic antiquity; for in it alone we find our hope of a renovation and purification of the German spirit through the fire-magic of music. What else shall we name, that amid the present desolation and fatigue of culture might awaken any comforting expectation for the future? We look in vain for one single vigorous root, for one spot of fruitful healthy soil: Everywhere dust, sand, torpidity, languor! Under such circum-stances a cheerless solitary wanderer could choose for himself no better symbol than the Knight with Death and the Devil, as Dürer has sketched him to us — the mail-clad knight, grim and stern of visage, who undisturbed by his gruesome companions, yet without hope, pursues his terrible path with horse and hound, alone. Our Schopenhauer was such a Dürerian knight: he was destitute of all hope, but he sought the truth. We have not his equal today.

But how suddenly this gloomily depicted wilderness of our exhausted culture changes when it is touched by the Dionysian magic! A hurri-cane seizes everything decrepit, decaying, broken, and stunted; enwraps it whirlingly in a red cloud of dust; and like a vulture carries it off into the air. Confused, we look for what has vanished: for what we see is something risen to the golden light as from a depression, so full and green, so luxuriantly vital, so ardent, so immeasurable. In the midst of this exuberance of life, sorrow and joy, Tragedy sits, in sublime ecstasy; she listens to a sad song, far away — it tells of the Mothers of Being, whose names are: *Wahn*, *Wille*, *Wehe*.[22] — Yes, my friends, have faith with me in Dionysian life and in the rebirth of tragedy. The time of the Socratic man is past: crown yourselves with ivy, take the thyrsus in your hand, and marvel not if tigers and panthers lie down fawning at your feet. Dare now to be tragic men, for ye shall be redeemed! Ye shall accompany the Dionysian festive procession from India to Greece! Arm yourselves for hard strife, but have faith in the wonders of your god!

---

[22] Whim, will, woe.

21

PASSING back from the hortatory tones to the mood befitting the contemplative man, I repeat that only from the Greeks can we learn what such a sudden and miraculous awakening of tragedy must signify for the inner fabric of a people's life. It is the people of the tragic mysteries who fight the battles with the Persians: and, conversely, the people who waged such wars required tragedy as a necessary healing potion. Who would have imagined that there was still such a uniformly powerful effusion of the simplest political sentiments, the most natural domestic instincts and the primitive manly delight in battle in this very people after it had been agitated so profoundly for several generations by the most violent convulsions of the Dionysian demon? If with every noteworthy extension of the Dionysian life one always perceives that the Dionysian release from the shackles of the individual makes itself felt first of all in an increased encroachment on the political instincts, to the extent of causing indifference, yea, even hostility, it is certain, on the other hand, that the state-forming Apollo is also the genius of the *principium individuationis*, and that the state and the domestic sentiment cannot survive without an assertion of the individual personality. For any people there is but one road leading from orgasm — the way to Indian Buddhism, which, that its longing for nothingness may be at all endured, requires those rare ecstatic states raised high above space, time, and the individual; just as these in turn demand a philosophy which teaches one how to overcome the indescribable depression of the intermediate states by means of the imagination. With the same necessity, owing to the unconditional domination of political impulses, a people drifts into a path of extremest secularization, whose most magnificent but also most terrible expression is the Roman *imperium*.

Placed between India and Rome, and constrained to a choice, misleading in either case, the Greeks succeeded in devising in classical purity still a third form, not indeed for long private use, but just on that account destined for immortality. — For it holds true in all things that those whom the gods love die young, but, on the other hand, it is equally certain that they can live eternally with the gods. One should not require the noblest things to possess the durable toughness of leather; the staunch durability, for instance, which was inherent in the Roman national character, probably does not belong to the indispensable predicates of perfection. But if we ask what medicinal means enabled the

Greeks, in their best period, despite the fury of their Dionysian and political impulses, neither to exhaust themselves in ecstatic brooding, nor in a consuming scramble for empire and worldly honor, but on the contrary to achieve the splendid mixture which we find in a noble, inflaming, and contemplatively disposing wine, we must remember the enormous power of *tragedy*, exciting, purifying, and releasing the entire life of a people; the highest value of which we shall divine only when, as with the Greeks, it presents itself as the essence of all the prophylactic healing forces, as the mediator arbitrating between the strongest and most inherently fateful characteristics of a people.

Tragedy absorbs into itself the highest musical ecstasy so that it absolutely brings music to perfection among the Greeks, as among ourselves; but it then places beside it tragic myth and the tragic hero. The latter, like a mighty Titan, takes the entire Dionysian world on his shoulders and relieves us of the burden; while, on the other hand, by means of this same tragic myth, tragedy is able through the tragic hero, to deliver us from the intense longing for this existence, and to remind us with warning hand of another existence and a higher joy, for which the struggling hero prepares himself presentiently by his destruction, not by his victories. Tragedy sets a sublime symbol, the myth, between the universal authority of its music and the receptive Dionysian hearer, and produces in him the illusion that music is only the most effective means for the animating, the plastic world of myth. Relying upon this noble illusion, she may now move her limbs for the dithyrambic dance, and abandon herself unhesitatingly to an orgiastic feeling of freedom, in which, as music itself, without this illusion, she could not venture to indulge. The myth, while protecting us from the music, on the other hand, affords it the highest freedom. By way of return, music imparts to tragic myth an impressive and convincing metaphysical significance such as could never be attained by word and image, without this unique aid; and the tragic spectator in particular experiences thereby the sure presentment of supreme joy to which the path through destruction and negation leads; so that he imagines he hears the innermost abyss of things speaking audibly to him.

If with these last propositions I have succeeded in giving perhaps only a preliminary expression, intelligible to few at first, to this difficult idea, I must not here desist from stimulating my friends to a further attempt, or cease from beseeching them to prepare themselves, by a detached example of our common experience, for the recognition of the more generous proposition. In this example I must not appeal to those who make use of the pictures of the scenic processes, the words and the emotions of the performers, to approximate musical perception; for none of these speak music as their mother-tongue, and despite these aids get no farther than the outer precincts of musical perception, without ever being allowed to touch its innermost shrines; some of them, like Gervinus, do not even reach the precincts by this path. But I must address myself only to those who, being immediately allied to music, have it as it were for their mother's breast and are connected with things almost exclusively by unconscious musical relations. I ask the question of these genuine musicians: can they imagine a man capable of hearing the third act of *Tristan und Isolde* without any aid of word or scenery, purely as a vast symphonic period, without expiring by a spasmodic distention of all the wings of the soul? A man who has thus, so to speak, put his ear to the heart-chamber of the world-will, who feels the furious desire for existence issuing from it as thundering stream or gently dispersed brook, into all the veins of the world, would he not collapse all at once? Could he endure, in the wretched fragile tenement of the human individual, to hear the re-echo of countless cries of joy and sorrow from the "vast void of cosmic night," without flying irresistibly towards his primitive home at the sound of this pastoral dance-song of metaphysics? But if, nevertheless, such a work can be heard as a whole, without a renunciation of individual existence, and if such a creation could be created without demolishing its creator, where are we to find the solution of this contradiction?

Here between our highest musical excitement and the music in question are interposed the tragic myth and the tragic hero — in reality only as symbols of the most universal facts, of which only music can speak directly. If, however, we felt as purely Dionysian beings, myth as a symbol would stand by us absolutely ineffective and unnoticed, and would never for a moment prevent us from giving ear to the re-echo of the *universalia ante rem*. Here, however, the *Apollonian* power, with a view to the restoration of the almost shattered individuals, bursts forth with the healing balm of the blissful illusion: all of a sudden we imagine we see only Tristan, motionless, asking himself dully: "The old tune, why does it wake me?" And what once moved us like a hollow sigh from the heart of being now seems to tell us only how "waste and empty is the sea." And whereas, breathless, we once thought to expire by a convulsive distention of all our feelings, and only a slender tie bound us to our present existence, we now hear and see only the hero wounded to death, yet not dying, with his despairing cry: "Longing! Longing! In death still longing! for very longing not dying!" And whereas, formerly after such an excess and superabundance of consuming agonies, the jubilation of the horn rent our hearts almost like the very extreme of agony, the rejoicing Kurwenal now stands between us and this "jubilation as such," his face turned toward the ship which carries Isolde. However powerfully we are touched by fellow-suffering, it nevertheless delivers us in a manner from the primordial suffering of the world, just as the symbol-image of the myth delivers us from the immediate perception of the highest world-idea, just as the thought and the word deliver us from the unchecked effusion of the unconscious will. The glorious Apollonian illusion makes it appear as if the very tone-world presented itself to us as a plastic cosmos, as if even the fate of Tristan and Isolde had been merely formed and molded therein as out of some most soft and yielding material.

Thus does the Apollonian tear us away from Dionysian universality and make us delight in individuals; to these it attaches our sympathetic emotion; through these it satisfies our sense of beauty which longs for great and sublime forms; it presents us with biographical portraits, and incites us to a thoughtful comprehension of the essence of life dwelling within them. With the immense combined power of the image, the concept, the ethical teaching and the sympathetic emotion — the Apollonian influence uplifts man from his orgiastic self-annihilation and deceives him concerning the universality of the Dionysian process into the belief that he is seeing a detached picture of the world (Tristan and Isolde for instance), and that, *through music*, he will be enabled to *see* it with still more essential clearness. What can the healing magic of Apollo not accomplish when it can even excite in us the illusion that the Dionysian is actually in the service of the Apollonian and is capable of enhancing its effects, in fact, that music is essentially the representative art for an Apollonian content?

By means of the pre-established harmony obtaining between per-fected drama and its music, the drama attains the highest degree of conspicuousness, such as is usually unattainable in mere spoken drama. As all the animated figures of the scene in the independently evolved lines of melody simplify themselves before us to the distinctness of a single curved line, the co-existence of these lines is also audible in the harmonic change which sympathizes in a most delicate manner as the process evolves: through which change the relations of things become immediately perceptible to us in a sensible and not at all abstract manner, as we likewise perceive that it is only in these relations that the essence of a character and of a melodic line manifests itself clearly. And while music thus compels us to a broader and more intensive vision than usual, and makes us spread out the curtain of the scene before our eyes like a delicate texture, the world of the stage is as infinitely ex-panded for our spiritualized, introspective eye as it is illumined out-wardly from within. How can the word-poet furnish anything analogous, who strives to attain this internal expansion and illumination of the visible stage-world by a much more imperfect mechanism and by an indirect method, proceeding as he does from word and concept? Although musical tragedy also avails itself of the word, it can at the same time place beside it its basis and origin, and can make clear to us the development of the word, from within outwards.

Concerning the process just described, however, we may still make the definite statement that it is only a glorious appearance, namely, the aforementioned Apollonian *illusion*, through whose influence we are to be delivered from the Dionysian obtrusion and excess. For, at bottom, the relation of music to drama is precisely the reverse; music is the essential idea of the world, drama is but the reflection of this idea, a detached adumbration of it. The identity between the melody and the living form, between the harmony and the character-relations of that form, is true in a sense opposite to what one would suppose on the contemplation of musical tragedy. We may agitate and enliven the form in the most conspicuous manner, and illuminate it from within, but it still remains merely a phenomenon, from which there is no bridge to lead us to the true reality, to the heart of the world. But out of this heart speaks music; and though countless phenomena of the kind might be passing manifestations of this music, they could never exhaust its essence, but would always be merely its externalized copies. Of course, as regards the intricate relation of music and drama, nothing can be explained, while everything may be confused by the popular and thoroughly false antithesis of soul and body; but the unphilosophical crudeness of this antithesis seems to have become — who knows for what reasons — a readily accepted Article of Faith with our estheticians, while they have learned nothing concerning an antithesis of the phenomenon and the thing-in-itself — or perhaps for equally unknown reasons they have not cared to learn anything about it.

Should our analysis have established the point that the Apollonian element in tragedy has by means of its illusion gained a complete victory over the Dionysian primordial element of music, and has made music itself subservient to its end, namely, the clearest possible elucidation of the drama, it would certainly be necessary to add a very important restriction: that at the most essential point this Apollonian illusion is dissolved and annihilated. The drama, which, aided by music, unfolds itself before us with such inwardly illumined distinctness in all its movements and figures, that we imagine we see the texture unfolding on the loom as the shuttle flies to and fro, — this drama attains as a whole an effect which *transcends all Apollonian artistic effects*. In the collective effect of tragedy, the Dionysian once again dominates. Tragedy closes with a sound which could never emanate from the realm of Apollonian art. And the Apollonian illusion thereby reveals itself as what it really is — the assiduous veiling during the performance of the tragedy of the intrinsically Dionysian effect: which, however, is so powerful, that it ends by forcing the Apollonian drama itself into a sphere where it begins to talk with Dionysian wisdom, and even denies itself and its Apollonian conspicuousness. So that the intricate relation of the Apollonian and the Dionysian in tragedy may really be symbolized by a fraternal union of the two deities: Dionysus speaks the language of Apollo; Apollo, however, finally speaks the language of Dionysus; and so the highest goal of tragedy and of art in general is attained.

22

LET the attentive friend picture to himself purely and simply, according to his experience, the effect of a true musical tragedy. I think I have so portrayed the phenomenon of this effect in both its phases that he will now know how to interpret his own experiences. For he will recollect that with regard to the myth which passed before him he felt himself exalted to a kind of omniscience, as if his visual faculty were no longer merely a surface faculty, but capable of penetrating into the interior, and as if he now saw before him, with the aid of music, the ebullitions of the will, the conflict of motives, and the swelling stream of the passions, almost sensibly visible, like a multitude of actively moving lines and figures; and he would feel as if he could thereby dip into the most delicate secrets of unconscious emotions. While he thus becomes conscious of the highest exaltation of his instincts for clarity and transfiguration, he nevertheless feels with equal definiteness that this long series of Apollonian artistic effects still does *not* generate that blessed continuance in will-less contemplation which the plastic artist and the epic poet, that is to say, the strictly Apollonian artists, evoke in him by their artistic productions: to wit, the justification of the world of the *individuatio* attained by this contemplation, — which is the climax and essence of Apollonian art. He beholds the transfigured world of the stage and nevertheless denies it. He sees the tragic hero before him in epic clearness and beauty, and nevertheless rejoices in his annihilation. He comprehends the action in the minutest detail, and yet loves to flee into the incomprehensible. He feels the actions of the hero to be justified, and is nevertheless still more elated when these actions annihilate their originator. He shudders at the sufferings which will befall the hero, and yet in them he anticipates a higher and much more overpowering joy. He sees more extensively and profoundly than ever, and yet wishes to be blind. Whence must we derive this curious internal dissension, this collapse of the Apollonian apex, if not from the *Dionysian* spell, which, though apparently exciting the Apollonian emotions to their highest pitch, can nevertheless force into its service this excess of Apollonian power? The *tragic myth* is to be understood only as a symbolizing of Dionysian wisdom through Apollonian art-media. The mythus conducts the world of phenomena to its boundaries, where it denies itself, and seeks to flee back again into the bosom of the true and only reality; where it then, like Isolde, seems to strike up its metaphysical swansong:

> "In des Wonnemeeres
> wogendem Schwall,
> in der Duft-Wellen
> tönendem Schall,
> in des Weltathems
> wehendem All —
> ertrinken — versinken —
> unbewusst — höchste Lust!"[23]

We may thus make real to ourselves through the experiences of the truly esthetic hearer the tragic artist himself as he creates his figures like a fecund divinity of individuation (in which sense his work can hardly be understood as an "imitation of nature") and when, on the other hand, his vast Dionysian impulse then absorbs this entire world of phenomena, in order to anticipate beyond it, and through its destruction, the highest artistic primal joy, in the bosom of the Primal Unity. Of course, our estheticians have nothing to say about this return in fraternal union of the two art-deities to the original home, nor of either the Apollonian or Dionysian excitement of the hearer, while they never tire of characterizing the struggle of the hero with fate, the triumph of the moral order of the world, or the purgation of the emotions through tragedy, as the properly Tragic: an indefatigability which makes me think that perhaps they are not esthetically sensitive men at all, but are to be regarded merely as moral beings when hearing tragedy. Never since Aristotle has an explanation of the tragic effect been offered, by which an esthetic activity of the hearer could be inferred from artistic circumstances. At one time pity and terror are supposed to be forced to an alleviating release through the serious action, at another time we are supposed to

---

[23] "In the sea of pleasure's Billowing roll, In the ether-wave's Ringing sound, In the world-breath's Drifting whole — To drown, to sink — Unconscious — extremest joy!"

feel elevated and inspired at the victory of good and noble principles, at the sacrifice of the hero in the interest of a moral conception of the universe; and however sure I am that for countless men precisely this, and only this, is the effect of tragedy, it just as plainly follows that all these men, together with their interpreting estheticians, have had no experience of tragedy as the highest *art*. The pathological discharge, the catharsis of Aristotle, which philologists are at a loss whether to include under medicinal or moral phenomena, recalls a remarkable anticipation of Goethe. "Without a lively pathological interest," he says, "I too have never yet succeeded in elaborating a tragic situation of any kind, and hence I have rather avoided than sought it. Can it perhaps have been still another of the merits of the ancients that the deepest pathos was with them merely esthetic play, whereas with us the truth of nature must co-operate in order to produce such a work?" we can now answer this latter profound question in the affirmative after our glorious experiences, in which we have found to our astonishment in the case of musical tragedy itself, that the deepest pathos can in reality be merely esthetic play; and therefore we are justified in believing that now for the first time the proto-phenomenon of the tragic can be described with some degree of success. He who now still persists in talking only of those vicarious effects proceeding from extra-esthetic spheres, and does not feel himself raised above the pathological-moral process may despair of his esthetic nature: for which we recommend to him, by way of inno-cent equivalent, the interpretation of Shakespeare after the fashion of Gervinus, and the diligent search for poetic justice.

Thus with the rebirth of tragedy the *esthetic hearer* is also reborn, in whose place in the theater a curious *quid pro quo* was wont to sit with half-moral and half-learned pretensions — the "critic." Everything in his sphere hitherto has been artificial and merely glossed over with a semblance of life. The performing artist in fact was at a loss as to how to deal with a hearer who comported himself so critically; hence he, as well as the dramatist or operatic composer who inspired him, searched anxiously for the last remains of life in a being so pretentiously barren and incapable of enjoyment. Such "critics," however, have hitherto constituted the public; the student, the schoolboy, even the most harm-less female, were already unwittingly prepared by education and by magazines for a similar perception of works of art. The nobler natures among the artists when dealing with such a public counted upon exciting their moral-religious emotions, and the appeal to the moral world-order operated vicariously, when actually some powerful artistic spell should have enraptured the true hearer. Or again, some imposing or at all events exciting trend of the contemporary political and social world was so vividly presented by the dramatist that the hearer could forget his critical exhaustion and abandon himself to similar emotions, as, in patriotic or war-like moments, or before the tribune of parliament, or at the condemnation of crime and vice — an estrangement of the true aims of art which could not but lead directly now and then to a cult of such tendencies. But here there took place what has always taken place with factitious arts, an extraordinarily rapid degeneration of these tendencies, so that, for instance, the tendency to use the theater as a means for the moral education of the people, which in Schiller's time was taken seriously, is already reckoned among the incredible antiquities of an abandoned culture. While the critic got the upper hand in the theater and concert-hall, the journalist in the school, and the press in society, art degenerated into a trivial topic of conversation, and esthetic criticism was used as a means of uniting a vain, distracted, selfish and moreover piteously unoriginal society, whose character is suggested by Schopenhauer's parable of the porcupines: with the result that art has never been so much talked about and so little esteemed. But is it still possible to have intercourse with a man capable of conversing on Beethoven or Shakespeare? Let each answer this question according to his own feelings: he will at any rate show by his answer his conception of "culture," provided he at least tries to answer the question, and has not already grown mute with astonishment.

On the other hand, many a being more nobly and delicately endowed by nature, though he may have gradually become a critical barbarian in the manner described, might have something to say of the unexpected as well as totally unintelligible effect which a successful performance of *Lohengrin*, for example, had on him: except that perhaps every warning and interpreting hand was lacking to guide him; so that the incomprehensibly diffused and quite incomparable sensation which then thrilled him remained isolated and became extinct, like a mysterious star after a short period of brilliance. But it was then that he had an inkling of what the esthetic hearer is.

23

HE who wishes to test himself rigorously as to whether he is related to the true esthetic hearer, or whether he belongs rather to the community of the Socratic-critical men, need only examine sincerely the feeling with which he accepts the *wonder* represented on the stage: whether he feels his historical sense, which insists on strict psychological causality, insulted by it, whether with benevolent concession he admits the wonder as a phenomenon intelligible to childhood, but alien to him, or whether he experiences anything else from it. For in this way he will be able to determine on the whole how capable he is of understanding *myth*, the concentrated picture of the world, which, as abbreviature of phenomena, cannot dispense with wonder. It is probable, however, that almost every one, upon close examination, feels so broken up by the critico-historical spirit of our culture, that he can only make the former existence of myth credible to himself by learned means through inter-mediary abstractions. Without myth, however, every culture loses its healthy creative natural power: it is only a horizon encompassed with myths that rounds off to unity a social movement. It is only myth that frees all the powers of the imagination and of the Apollonian dream from their aimless wanderings. The mythical figures have to be the unnoticed omnipresent genii, under whose care the young soul grows to maturity, by the signs of which the man gives meaning to his life and struggles: and the state itself knows no more powerful unwritten law than the mythical foundation which vouches for its connection with religion and its growth from mythical ideas.

On the other hand, let us now think of the abstract man unguided by myth, the abstract education, the abstract morality, the abstract justice, the abstract state: let us picture to ourselves the lawless roving of the artis-tic imagination, unchecked by native myth: let us imagine a culture which has no fixed and sacred primitive seat, but is doomed to exhaust all its possibilities, and to nourish itself wretchedly on all other cultures — there we have the Present, the result of Socratism, which is bent on the destruction of myth. And now the mythless man remains eternally hun-gering amid the past, and digs and grubs for roots, though he have to dig for them even among the remotest antiquities. The terrible historical need of our unsatisfied modern culture, the assembling around one of countless other cultures, the consuming desire for knowledge — what does all this point to, if not to the loss of myth, the loss of the mythical home, the mythical maternal bosom? Let us ask ourselves whether the feverish and uncanny excitement of this culture is anything but the eager seizing and snatching at food of hungry man — and who would care to contribute anything more to a culture which cannot be satisfied no matter how much it devours, and at whose contact the most vigorous and wholesome nourishment habitually changes into "history and criticism"?

We should also have to regard our German character with sorrowful despair, if it had already become inextricably entangled in, or even identi-cal with this culture, as we may observe to our horror is the case in civi-lized France; and that which for a long time was the great advantage of

France and the cause of her vast superiority, to wit, this very identity of people and culture, might compel us at the sight thereof to congratulate ourselves that this so questionable culture of ours has hitherto had nothing in common with the noble heart of our people's character. On the contrary, all our hopes stretch out longingly towards the perception that beneath this restlessly palpitating civilized life and educational convulsion there is concealed a glorious, intrinsically healthy, primitive power, which, to be sure, stirs vigorously only at intervals in stupendous moments, and then continues to dream of future awakening. It is from this abyss that the German Reformation came forth: in the choral-hymn of which the future melody of German music first resounded. So deep, courageous, and spiritual, so exuberantly good and tender did this chorale of Luther sound — as the first Dionysian luring call breaking forth from dense thickets at the approach of spring. To it responded with emulative echo the solemnly wanton procession of Dionysian revelers, to whom we are indebted for German music — and to whom we shall be indebted for *the rebirth of German myth.*

I know that I must now lead the sympathizing and attentive friend to an elevated position of lonesome contemplation, where he will have but few companions, and I call out encouragingly to him that we must hold fast to our shining guides, the Greeks. That we might clarify our esthetic knowledge, we previously borrowed from them the two divine forms, each of whom rules over a separate realm of art, and concerning whose mutual contact and exaltation we acquired a notion through Greek tragedy. Through a remarkable disruption of both these primitive artistic impulses, the ruin of Greek tragedy seemed to be necessarily brought about: with which process a degeneration and a transformation of the Greek national character was quite in keeping, summoning us to earnest reflection as to how closely and necessarily art and the people, myth and custom, tragedy and the state, are rooted together. The ruin of tragedy was at the same time the ruin of myth. Until then the Greeks had been involuntarily compelled to connect all experiences at once with their myths: indeed it was only through this association that they could understand them, so that even the most immediate present necessarily appeared to them *sub specie æterni* and in a certain sense as timeless. Into this current of the timeless, however, the state as well as art plunged in order to find repose from the burden and eagerness of the moment. A people — and, for that matter, also a man — is to be valued only according to its ability to impress on its experiences the stamp of eternity: for it is thus, as it were, desecularized; thus it reveals its unconscious inner conviction of the relativity of time and of the true, that is, the metaphysical significance of life. The contrary happens when a people begins to comprehend itself historically and to demolish the mythical bulwarks surrounding it: with which there is usually connected a marked secularization, a break with the unconscious metaphysics of its earlier existence, with all its ethical consequences. Greek art and especially Greek tragedy delayed above all the annihilation of myth: it was necessary to annihilate these also to be able to live detached from the native soil, unbridled in the wilderness of thought, custom, and deed. Even then this metaphysical impulse still endeavors to create for itself a form of apotheosis (weakened, no doubt) in the Socratism of science that urges to life: but in its lower stage the same impulse led only to a feverish search, which gradually lost itself in a pandemonium of myths and superstitions accumulated from all quarters: in the midst of which, nevertheless, the Hellene sat with a yearning heart till he contrived, as Græculus, to mask his fever with Greek cheerfulness and Greek levity, or to narcotize himself completely with some gloomy Oriental superstition.

We have been approaching this state in the most striking manner since the reawakening of Alexandrian-Roman antiquity in the fifteenth century, after a long, most easily describable, interlude. On the heights there is the same exuberant love of knowledge, the same insatiate happiness of the discoverer, the same tremendous secularization, and, with these, a homeless wandering, an eager intrusion at strange tables, a frivolous deification of the present or a dull senseless estrangement, all *sub specie sæculi*, of the present time: which same symptoms lead one to infer the same defect at the heart of this culture, the destruction of myth. It seems hardly possible to transplant a foreign myth with permanent success, without fatally injuring the tree which may occasionally be sufficiently strong and healthy to eliminate the foreign element after a terrible struggle; but which must ordinarily consume itself in a languishing and stunted condition or in a sickly luxuriance. So highly do we rate the pure and vigorous kernel of the German character that from it alone may we venture to expect this elimination of forcibly ingrafted foreign elements, and we deem it possible that the German spirit will reflect anew on itself. Perhaps many will be of opinion that this spirit must begin its struggle with the elimination of the Romanic element. Such people may recognize an external preparation for, and encouragement of, this struggle in the victorious bravery and bloody glory of the late war; but must seek the inner constraint in the emulative zeal to be eternally worthy of our sublime protagonists on this path, of Luther as well as of our great artists and poets. But let him never think he can fight such battles without the household gods, without his mythical home, without a "restoration" of all things German! And if the German should be looking around timidly for a guide to lead him back to his long-lost home, whose ways and paths he hardly knows any longer — let him but listen to the ecstatic luring call of the Dionysian bird, which hovers above him, and would fain point the way for him.

24

AMONG the peculiar artistic effects of musical tragedy we had to emphasize an Apollonian *illusion*, through which we are to be saved from an immediate oneness with the Dionysian music, while our musical excitement is able to discharge itself on an Apollonian domain and in an interposed visible middle world. It therefore seemed to us that precisely through this discharge this middle world of theatrical procedure, the drama generally, became visible and intelligible from within in a degree unattainable in all other forms of Apollonian art: so that here, where this art was as if winged and borne aloft by the spirit of music, we had to recognise the highest exaltation of its powers, and consequently, in the fraternal union of Apollo and Dionysus, the climax of the Apollonian as well as of the Dionysian artistic aims.

Of course, the Apollonian light-picture did not, precisely with this inner illumination through music, attain the peculiar effect of the weaker forms of Apollonian art. What the epos and the animated stone can do — constrain the contemplative eye to calm delight in the world of the *individuatio* — could not be realized here, notwithstanding a greater animation and distinctness. We contemplated the drama and penetrated with piercing glance into its inner agitated world of motives — and yet it seemed as if only a symbolic picture passed before us whose deepest meaning we almost believed we had divined, and which we desired to draw aside like a curtain in order to behold the original behind it. The greatest distinctness of the picture did not suffice us: for it seemed to reveal as well as veil something; and while with its symbolic revelation it seemed to invite the rending of the veil for the disclosure of the mysterious background, this illuminated all-consciousness itself enthralled the eye and prevented it from penetrating more deeply.

He who has not experienced this — to be constrained to view, and at the same time to long for something beyond the viewing — will hardly be able to conceive how clearly and definitely these two processes co-exist and are felt to co-exist in the contemplation of tragic myth; while the truly esthetic spectators will confirm my assertion that among the peculiar effects of tragedy this conjecture is the most noteworthy. Now let this phenomenon of the esthetic spectator be transferred to an analogous process in the tragic artist, and the genesis of *tragic myth* will have been understood. It shares with the Apollonian sphere of art the full delight in appearance and contemplation, and at the same time it denies this delight and finds a still higher satisfaction in the annihilation of the visible world of appearance. The substance of the tragic myth is first of all an epic event involving the glorification of the fighting hero: but how does it come about that the essentially puzzling trait, the suffering of the hero, the most painful victories, the most agonizing contrasts of motives, in short, the exemplification of the wisdom of Silenus, or, in esthetic terms, the ugly and unharmonious, are always represented anew in such countless and popular forms, and precisely at the most youthful and exuberant age of a people, unless there is really a higher delight experienced in all this?

For the fact that in life things actually take such a tragic course would hardly explain the original of a form of art; provided that art is not merely an imitation of the reality of nature, but in fact a metaphysical supplement to the reality of nature, placed beside it for purpose of conquest. Tragic myth, in so far as it really belongs to art, also fully participates in this transfiguring metaphysical purpose of art in general. What does it transfigure, however, when it presents the phenomenal world under the form of the suffering hero? Least of all the "reality" of this phenomenal world, for it says to us: "Look at this! Look carefully! It is your life! It is the hour-hand of the clock of your existence!"

And myth has displayed this life, in order thereby to transfigure it for us? If not, how shall we account for the esthetic pleasure with which even these representations are accompanied? I am inquiring concerning the esthetic pleasure, and am well aware that besides this pleasure many of these representations may occasionally create even a moral delectation, perhaps in the form of pity or of a moral triumph. But he who would derive the effect of the tragic exclusively from these moral sources, as indeed was usually the case far too long in esthetics, let him not think that he has done anything for Art thereby; for above all Art must insist on purity in her domain. The very first requirement for the explanation of tragic myth is that its characteristic pleasure must be sought in the purely esthetic sphere, without encroaching on the domain of pity, fear, or the morally sublime. How can the ugly and the unharmonious, the substance of tragic myth, excite esthetic pleasure?

Here it becomes necessary to raise ourselves with one daring bound into a metaphysics of Art. Therefore I repeat my former proposition that only as an esthetic phenomenon may existence and the world appear justified: and in this sense it is precisely the function of tragic myth to convince us that even the ugly and unharmonious is an artistic game which the will plays with itself in the eternal fullness of its joy. But this not easily comprehensible proto-phenomenon of Dionysian art becomes, in a direct way, singularly intelligible, and is immediately apprehended in the wonderful significance of *musical dissonance:* just as in general it is music alone, placed in contrast to the world, which can give us an idea as to what is meant by the justification of the world as an esthetic phenomenon. The joy aroused by the tragic myth has the same origin as the joyful sensation of dissonance in music. The Dionysian, with its primordial joy experienced in pain itself, is the common source of music and tragic myth.

Is it not possible that by calling to our aid the musical relation of dissonance, we may meanwhile have essentially facilitated the difficult problem of the tragic effect? For we now understand what it means to wish to view tragedy and at the same time to have a longing beyond that viewing: a frame of mind, which, referring to the artistically employed dissonance, we should have to characterize simply by saying that we desire to hear and at the same time have a longing beyond the hearing. That striving for the infinite, the beating wings of longing accompanying the highest delight in the clearly perceived reality, remind us that in both states we must recognize a Dionysian phenomenon, which reveals to us again and again the playful construction and demolishing of the world of individuals as the overflow of a primitive delight, just as Heraclitus the Obscure compares the world-building power to a playing child which places stones here and there and builds sandhills only to overthrow them again.

Hence, in order to form a true estimate of the Dionysian capacity of a people, we must think not only of their music, but equally of their tragic myth, the second witness of this capacity. Considering this close relationship between music and myth, we may now in like manner infer that a degeneration and depravation of the one involves a deterioration of the other: if it is at all true that the weakening of the myth is generally indicative of a debilitation of the Dionysian capacity. Concerning both, however, a glance at the development of the German genius should not leave us in any doubt; in the opera just as in the abstract character of our mythless existence, in an art degenerated to pastime as well as in a life guided by concepts, the inartistic as well as life-consuming nature of Socratic optimism had revealed itself to us. For our consolation, however, there have been some indications that nevertheless in some inaccessible abyss the German spirit still rests and dreams, undestroyed, in glorious health, profundity, and Dionysian strength, like a knight sunk in slumber: from which abyss the Dionysian song rises to our ears to let us know that this German knight even now is dreaming his primitive Dionysian myth in blissfully earnest visions. Let no one believe that the German spirit has forever lost its mythical home when it can still understand so plainly the voices of the birds which tell of that home. Some day it will find itself awake in all the morning freshness following a deep sleep: then it will slay the dragons, destroy the malignant dwarfs, waken Brünnhilde — and Wotan's spear itself will be unable to obstruct its course!

My friends, ye who believe in Dionysian music, ye also know what tragedy means to us. There we have tragic myth reborn from music — and in this birth we can hope for everything and forget what is most afflicting. What is most afflicting to all of us, however, is — the prolonged degradation in which the German genius has lived estranged from house and home in the service of malignant dwarfs. Ye understand my words — as ye will also, in conclusion, understand my hopes.

25

MUSIC and tragic myth are equally the expression of the Dionysian capacity of a people, and are inseparable from each other. Both originate in a sphere of art lying beneath and beyond the Apollonian; both transfigure a region in whose joyous harmony all dissonance, like the terrible picture of the world, dies charmingly away; both play with the sting of displeasure, relying on their most potent magic; both thereby justify the existence even of the "worst world." Here the Dionysian, as compared with the Apollonian, exhibits itself as the eternal and original artistic force, which in general calls into existence the entire world of phenomena; in the midst of which a new transfiguring appearance becomes necessary, in order to keep alive the animated world of individuation. If we could conceive of an incarnation of dissonance — and what else is man? — then, that it might live, this dissonance would need a glorious illusion to cover its features with a veil of beauty. This is the true artistic function of Apollo: in whose name we include all the countless manifestations of the fair realm of illusion, which at each moment render life in general worth living and impel one to the experience of the next moment.

At the same time, just as much of this basis of all existence — the Dionysian substratum of the world — is allowed to enter into the consciousness of human beings, as can be surmounted again by the Apollonian transfiguring power, so that these two art-impulses are compelled to develop their powers in strictly mutual proportion, according to the law of eternal justice. When the Dionysian powers rise with such strength as we are experiencing at present, there can be no doubt that, wrapped in a cloud, Apollo has already descended to us; whose fullest and most beautiful effects a coming generation may perhaps behold.

That this effect is necessary, however, each one would most surely perceive intuitively, if once he found himself carried back — even in a dream — into an Old-Hellenic existence. Walking under high Ionic colonnades, looking up towards a horizon defined by clear and noble lines, with reflections of his transfigured form by his side in shining marble, and around him solemnly marching or quietly moving men, with harmonious voices and rhythmical pantomime — in the presence of this perpetual influx of beauty would he not have to raise his hand to Apollo and exclaim: "Blessed race of Hellenes! How great Dionysus must be among you, when the Delian god deems such charms necessary to cure you of your dithyrambic madness!" To such a one, however, an aged Athenian, looking up to him with the sublime eyes of Æschylus, might answer: "Say also this, thou curious stranger: what must this people have suffered, that they might become thus beautiful! But now follow me to a tragic play, and sacrifice with me in the temple of both the deities!"